SHELLEY'S BOAT

Shelley's Boat

JULIAN ROACH

Harbour

This edition published for the first time in 2005 by
Harbour Books Ltd
20 Castlegate, York YO1 9RP
publicity@harbourbooks.co.uk
www.harbourbooks.co.uk

UK and Ireland sales by Signature
20 Castlegate, York YO1 9RP
Tel 01904 633633   Fax 01904 675445
sales@signaturebooks.co.uk

UK and European distribution by Orca Book Services
Stanley House, 3 Fleets Lane, Poole, Dorset BH15 3AJ
Tel 01202 665432   Fax 01202 666219
orders@orcabookservices.co.uk

A catalogue record for this book is
available from the British Library.

ISBN 1 905128 03 7

Typeset by Antony Gray
Printed and bound in Finland by WS Bookwell

FOR SWB

Acknowledgements

Without the cheerful encouragement of Steve Powell I might never have started and without his tireless and disciplined editorial help would probably never have stopped. It is much more of a pleasure than a duty to record my debt to him. My thanks go to Rosey Gray for curry-combing the text with rare and assiduous skill and weeding out errors. Those that remain will be the ones I have perversely put back in. Thanks, too, to Louise Perrin of the Russell-Cotes Museum, Bournemouth for bringing the museum's model of *Ariel* out of store for me to spend an afternoon with. Like many another harmless drudge, writer or insomniac, I owe much thanks to that great philanthropist Tim Berners-Lee for inventing the World Wide Web and to Google for their search engine; not least amongst many other benefits has been a huge saving on bus fares and postage stamps.

One

Wherever the English language is known, their names are known. They are known to be poets and, better yet, to be just what poets ought to be. Shelley and Byron stand to poetry where Mozart and Schubert stand to music: brilliant, effortless, prolific geniuses romantically marked for early death. There is a curious difference. Anybody who has been touched by the culture of the Western world will have heard at least some Mozart or Schubert, whether they knew it or not, while most of the millions who know the names of Byron or Shelley will never have read a line of their verse. Music has an advantage. You may need a certain amount of apparatus to make it but you don't even need to know a scale to enjoy it. To enjoy poetry you need to begin with a little more apparatus of language and culture.

And yet.

It would be strange to hear an actor or a lover, however soulful, described as Schubertian and, as far as I know, whole communities have not set out to live as Mozart lived, either literally or just as a fashion statement. On the other hand, it will not be long before you hear yet another actor with come-to-bed eyes and a sceptical smile described as Byronic, while the great revolution of my youth was the result of an entire generation deciding to be Shelley when they grew up. Or, rather, when they didn't, as a major aim of the sixties' 'Revolution' was to abolish growing up, along with all its associated forms of economic and political tyranny, replacing these things with art, communal possessions, free love, lots of hair and a regime of frequent hallucinations. Shelley was there first.

A widely discussed problem in the sixties was what to do with people over thirty, as they could never be anything but an oppressive gerontocracy, too far gone for any kind of re-education. We didn't worry about getting there ourselves. Somehow or other, like Shelley, we weren't going to.

Shelley ducked out of getting to thirty by drowning with one month to go when his badly, if beautifully, conceived boat, badly managed, met an entirely predictable storm. He remains the only poet to have met his death in a perfect metaphor for his life.

*   *   *

Nobody could say Death sneaked up on Shelley. It did not come in disguise or by stealth but in as noisy and obvious a form as it could. It came as a squalling thunderstorm of the kind so often, and so predictably, cradled on such a coast. Nature has her patterns, and the storm that closed the sweltering afternoon of the 8th of July 1822 followed a pattern familiar to all Ligurians. Or Floridians, come to that. It was all over in much less than an hour.

That afternoon, Shelley set out from Pisa's port of Livorno in the little yacht he'd first called *Don Juan* but now – being out of love with things Byronic – preferred to call *Ariel*. Some sailors, of course, think it unlucky to change a ship's name. It was a sail of forty miles or so northwards along the coast to Lerici, the little harbour from which he would be able to see, on the opposite curve of the bay, the cluster of roofs around the church of San Terenzo and, a little apart, the curious and solitary white house that he had left just a week before.

For all that he had spent much time floating around on lakes and rivers, Shelley had picked up no great practical understanding of boats and sails and sea. But then, for Shelley, sailing was not a thing to do, it was a place to be. He liked to be aboard and afloat, severed from the banal and the mundane. What he liked to do then was to read. Or write. He had told his new friend Trelawny that it was quite possible for him to handle the tiller and read poetry at the same time, 'as one was an intellectual activity and the other purely mechanical'. Edward Trelawny knew enough about these things to know better. As a boy of twelve and a brand-new midshipman with Admiral Duckworth's squadron, he had joined the fleet off Cadiz only a few weeks after the Battle of Trafalgar. The way Trelawny told it, of course, you'd have thought the decks were still smoking and hot with blood as he stepped aboard. He talked big, Trelawny, but then there was a genuine bigness about him. It was true, anyway, that his name had been there on the muster-roll of HMS *Colossus* when she had been paid off and no ship of Nelson's fleet had won greater glory than mighty *Colossus*, engaged for a long hour with no fewer than three of the enemy's line-of-battle. He might only have been transferred to her crew for the homeward voyage to Chatham, but he had stepped ashore on to the soil of England with the saviours of the nation, heroes of a stamp in the public mind that England would not know again until 1940. Still, you wouldn't have needed quite those naval qualifications to know that Shelley was wrong about helming and reading at the same time.

Shelley had two companions aboard as *Ariel* set off into a thickening and sultry haze. One was Edward Williams, a friend of little more than a year's standing who shared with Trelawny, and many another who came close to Shelley, an admiration that ran almost to worship. Shelley, in return, admired and envied the beauty of Edward's relationship with his extraordinarily lovely wife Jane. Shelley's admiration did not inhibit the idea that their relationship would be even more perfect if it were more triangular. Mary was silent, while Jane was sweetly singing. Mary was fraught and untouchable, while Jane soothed his pains with her 'magnetic' gifts and healing fingers. By night, beneath the stars, those same beautiful fingers strummed the guitar that he had given her, accompanied by the eternal beat of the sea. How could he not have come, lately and secretly, to be writing yearning and passionate verses to Jane?

The third soul aboard the little yacht, Charles Vivian, had been a member of the crew that had delivered her from her Genoese builders' yard a little less than two months earlier. He had stayed on at San Terenzo as a useful boat-hand for the summer, living in that bare, white, half-ruinous box of a house on the sea's edge that Shelley and Mary and Edward and Jane had taken for the summer. Young Charles was, perhaps, an early incarnation of a type now found in every marina where the sun shines: the boat bum, a nautical backpacker, young and fit, ready and able to do the grunting work in return for his keep, for the pleasure of knocking about the world and for the chance of meeting interesting people. Jumping ashore from *Don Juan* at the tiny harbour of Lerici, Charles was jumping into the chance of meeting some famously interesting people. Probably he'd been ready enough to step forward when hands were wanted to deliver Shelley's boat.

You might expect a boat newly built in Genoa to be delivered by a crew of Genoese but the three men who brought her down the coast, round the headland of Porto Venere and across the lovely bay to Lerici, were all Englishmen. This is not as surprising as it at first appears. The long Napoleonic Wars had ended and it was not just the English milord who was again free to follow his old habit of heading for balmier climes.

A quarter of a century of war had taken many plainer Englishmen as sailors and soldiers to bluer waters and warmer climes. Captain Roberts, for instance, the agent who'd acted for both Shelley and Byron in getting boats built in Genoa, was perhaps one of the many beached officers who found that their half-pay was a better wage abroad. Given that Trelawny, the midshipman, allowed himself to be called a lieutenant, it may well be that Roberts's promotion was also something of a social commission, not recorded in Whitehall. He may have been one of the fourteen hundred or so 'passed-midshipmen' – that is, midshipmen who had passed the examination for lieutenant – who were made up to lieutenant at the end of the wars by way of sending them off with a pension. His half-pay, then, would have been ninety-one pounds and five shillings a year: close to penury in England, much nearer to respectability in Genoa. Edward Trelawny had never really had his foot on the ladder to lieutenant and so had no half-pay, just three hundred a year from his family. He also claimed to be a deserter, which would have been good reason for the expatriate life had it been true, which it certainly wasn't. Either of these men might competently have taken *Don Juan* down the coast, save that both were far too busy supervising the completion of Lord Byron's commission, the much larger and fancier *Bolivar*.

It seems, though, that there was no difficulty in finding three other Englishmen for the job. Shelley – a mere baronet – may not have been a great lord and public spectacle, like Byron, and it was true that hardly anybody, let alone expatriate deckhands, had read his poetry, but he was notorious, all the same.

One of the reasons he was so little read was that, often as not, what he wrote could only be published in England in bold defiance of the laws against blasphemy or 'seditious libel'. One William Clarke had issued a pirated edition of *Queen Mab* and in 1822 was being prosecuted by the Society for the Suppression of Vice. He was to be jailed for four months. Richard Carlile, that obstinately courageous and unfairly forgotten hero of the long struggle for liberty, was another publisher to be thrown into jail for publishing, among many other things offensive to the government, extracts from the works of Shelley.

These things added nothing to Shelley's income and little to his fame as a poet but they did give him the blessing of a certain notoriety. He was not just Shelley the atheist but Shelley the proscribed anti-monarchist and revolutionary as well. He was Shelley the man so depraved that he was deemed by the Lord Chancellor to be unfit for the custody of his own children. He was Shelley the wild radical who lived – a former servant had said so – with a seraglio of women who were his sexual slaves.

So it is not surprising that three Englishmen stepped up for the job of delivering the boat and maybe catching sight of the notorious Mr Shelley. It is even less surprising that the eighteen-year-old Charles Vivian took the chance of staying with the boat, and with the interesting Mr Shelley's house party, for the summer.

A space must have been found for him in the upper quarters with the servants. Perhaps he found himself quartered with 'Il Barboso', Tita Falcieri, one of Lord Byron's men, lately run out of Pisa after being briefly imprisoned on a grievous bodily harm charge. Mary found him charming, diligent and honest and was sure of his innocence. He certainly had style. While in jail he threw a banquet for his fellow inmates. He must have had other likeable qualities, too. After Byron's death, he came to England and was found a place in the household of the poet's great friend, John Cam Hobhouse. Like Napoleon before him, Tita was struck by the beauty of English women but found English society odd. 'So serious, so well ordered that they make a playful Italian despair.' It was, he said, 'like living in a convent, they come to eat at the sound of a bell'.

So, even if there was no truth in the GBH charge, it is a fair guess that Tita got the choice of beds and that Charles did not argue. Then, why would he? He was a footloose, adventurous boy who brought nothing with him into the world of Casa Magni, with no ties and no reason to care for tomorrow. Except that, from the moment he stepped ashore in Lerici, he had just fifty-seven tomorrows remaining to him.

Shelley's Boat

For Tita, Casa Magni must at least have been an improvement on the jail at Pisa but Charles must have been surprised by the rough and ready quarters he found in San Terenzo. If the house was something more than a comfortable cottage in size, it was a great deal less in most other ways. It was in that state of abandoned neglect that becomes ruinous in a few seasons, especially when, as Mary Shelley put it, a house has 'its feet in the sea'.

Trelawny, revisiting the house after laying Shelley's ashes to rest in Rome, paints a characteristically vivid picture.

I arrived early at Lerici, and determined to sleep there, and finish my journey to Genoa on the following day. In the evening I walked to the Villa Magni . . . and the ground floor having neither door nor window, I walked in . . . I mounted the stairs or rather ladder into the dining-room they had lived in, for this and four small bedrooms were all the space they had. As I surveyed its splatchy walls, broken floor, cracked ceiling, and poverty-struck appearance, while I noted the loneliness of the situation, and remembered the fury of the waves that in blowing weather lashed its walls, I did not marvel at Mrs Shelley's and Mrs Williams's groans on first entering it; nor that it required all Ned Williams's persuasive powers to induce them to stop there. We men had only looked at the sea and scenery, and would have been satisfied with a tent. But women look to a house as their empire. Ladies without a drawing-room are like pictures without frames, or birds without feathers; knowing this they set to work with a will, and transformed it into a very pleasant abode.

Shelley's Boat

You would be forgiven for thinking, as Trelawny stands there, steeped in recollection, seeing it all again, that many years had passed. In fact, this is a poignant pause in his journey to Genoa to join Byron's expedition to Greece. Not twelve months had passed since he had come to that room to tell those women that the time for hope had gone. By the time he set sail with Byron on July 15th of 1823, just a year and a week would have passed since Shelley's death. Casa Magni, as he saw it then, was pretty much what it had been when he and Williams had found it. Whatever efforts Mary and Jane had made, and furniture apart, it was, then, pretty much the house as young Charles Vivian found it. He and the other servants, after all, lived in the attic where Jane and Mary's home-making had never reached. All they seem to have complained of up there, like the prisoners of Venice chained beneath the tiles of the Doge's palace, was the terrible heat.

The house stands today, neatly kept and respectably tenanted. Seen from any distance or from seaward, it is not much changed, though its feet are no longer quite in the sea. Modern San Terenzo has come to embrace the Casa Magni and sprawl a little beyond it towards Lerici. A road now runs between the house and the water's edge where, once upon a time, the traveller would have kept his feet dry by walking inside the arches of its terrace, as through a little cloister. The Trieste pizzeria and guest-house stands on one side, separated by a lane. On the other side, small apartment blocks step along the seafront for a hundred metres or so to the sanatorium, a larger building trying to disguise its want of charm with a coat of bright ochre paint. The sanatorium bridges the road with the limb of an upper storey, reaching on to a promontory that would otherwise have been too small to notice and so making a kind of southern gateway at the end of San Terenzo.

It is still a tiny place. In 1822, it hardly amounted to a village and Casa Magni stood outside it in isolation. Sand and shells had been washed or blown through its five arches into a ground floor fit only for the storage of boats and tackle. The terrace above those arches is still almost a jetty into the Mediterranean. Then, it would have seemed exactly that. Charles Vivian, or most of us today, might have thought it just the kind of place a poet would choose. In fact, it had been a case of *faute de mieux*. This coast had always been poor. After the long war and the years of high tax and famine that followed, it was poverty stricken. A decent house had been hard to find.

Two

It was Trelawny and Williams who had done most of the scouting for a place on the coast to spend the summer. By the time they came across the Casa Magni they had almost given up.

> Williams and I rode along the coast to the Gulf of Spezzia. Shelley had no pride or vanity to provide for, yet we had the greatest difficulty in finding any house in which the humblest civilised family could exist.
>
> On the shores of this superb bay, only surpassed in its natural beauty and capability by that of Naples, so effectually has tyranny paralysed the energies and enterprise of man, that the only indication of human habitation was a few most miserable fishing villages scattered along the margin of the bay. Near its centre, between the villages of Sant'Arenzo and Lerici, we came upon a lonely and abandoned building called the Villa Magni, though it looked more like a boat- or bathing-house than a place to live in.

Trelawny writes as he speaks and perhaps there is something of a Cornish burr in that delightful addition of a new saint to the Italian calendar, 'Sant'Arenzo'. On the other hand, this is also how Mary writes the saint's name, so perhaps it reflects the burr of what Mary would later call the 'detestable dialect' spoken by the locals. Either way, the house that lay near San Terenzo's little church did not offer much.

It consisted of a terrace or ground-floor unpaved, and used for storing boat-gear and fishing-tackle, and of a single storey over it divided into a hall or saloon and four small rooms which had once been whitewashed; there was one chimney for cooking. This place we thought the Shelleys might put up with for the summer. The only good thing about it was a verandah facing the sea, and almost over it. So we sought the owner and made arrangements, dependent on Shelley's approval, for taking it for six months. As to finding a palazzo grand enough for a Milordo Inglese, within a reasonable distance of the bay, it was out of the question.

The Milordo Inglese, of course, was Byron, who settled instead for summer quarters in a somewhat bourgeois villa outside Livorno, without relinquishing the more fitting palazzo in Pisa where he lived in the constant company of his present mistress, the Countess Guiccioli, together with her father (which made it more respectable) and his usual bizarre and unruly entourage of toffs, toughs and wild animals. Nowhere for Byron then, but somewhere for Percy and Mary and Edward and Jane and, at least for a while, Mary's stepsister, whose given names were Mary Jane but who, luckily, had taken to calling herself Claire. It was Claire's constant presence in the Shelley household – she had travelled with them when they eloped – that had given rise to the tales of a 'seraglio'.

These tales were not the less credible for the fact that six years before she set eyes on Casa Magni – almost to the day –

she had flung herself at Byron, conceiving a child with him, almost – indeed, quite possibly – at first meeting. By the time Byron left England, within a month of meeting her, their relationship amounted to rather more than a one-night stand, but not much more. Even by Byron's standards, it was a bad month for other business, with his wife forcing on him a legal separation that he did not want and that he resented bitterly. His last, disgusted, act of any meaning in England had been to sign the paper. The moments spared for the company of a lively eighteen-year-old, besotted by his fame and unequivocally eager to bed him, must have been moments of agreeable relief, but, to him, of little importance. For Claire, serving up her virginity with a kind of headlong urgency, those moments shaped her life for ever. Before quitting England, Byron had decided that she was over-excited, importunate and deluded. He'd been through all that and more with Caroline Lamb and did not care for it.

So he had been dismayed to see her lying in wait, with the Shelleys, in Geneva, just three months later. He was even more dismayed when he learned the special reason for her eagerness to catch up with him. All the same, he had acknowledged and agreed to provide for – as it would turn out – his daughter. The proviso was that she should live under his roof, and not with Claire, with whom he wanted no further intimacy. For the daughter's good, the mother eventually had yielded with a breaking heart. It was a heart that flew into distraction when she learned that Byron had placed Allegra in the keeping of nuns in a convent near Ravenna. She was convinced that the moral condition of women in Catholic Italy amounted more or less to depravity.

Shelley's Boat

The idea that her daughter would be turned into an Italian Catholic horrified her. For Byron, Catholicism was much better than the alternative of Claire's religion, which he believed to be none at all. As he wrote to Moore, just about the time the trouble blew up,

> . . . I am no enemy to religion, but the contrary. As a proof, I am educating my natural daughter a strict Catholic in a convent of Romagna; for I think people can never have *enough* of religion, if they are to have any. I incline, myself, very much to the Catholic doctrines . . .

If this is not entirely humbug, it is sanctimonious and self-serving. The truth about Allegra was that, at the age of three, she had become more of a handful than Byron's servants could easily cope with. More to the point, she was the reminder, increasingly vivid, noisy and eye-catching as the days passed, of complications in her father's history. She was a reminder on which Countess Guiccioli found she could not look with complacency.

In Italy, the convent offered a perfectly orthodox way of coping with this kind of thing. Many religious houses made a speciality of the business and Byron paid twice the going rate to ensure that she was cared for well. That meant little to Claire, who begged and pleaded for the return of her child. When begging failed she had begun to make crazy plans for kidnap. The scheme would have called for Shelley to forge a letter, and while Shelley was a man to take an unorthodox line in most things, even he was shocked by the madness of this idea. He sternly talked her out of it.

As they moved into Casa Magni, Shelley had news of

Allegra to give to Claire. Byron had written to him with it a week before but, with all the upheaval of uprooting themselves from Pisa, he'd thought it wiser to sit on it until they had moved in. Best that she should be nowhere near Lord Byron, for fear of what she might do.

Mary left Pisa with Claire by land while Shelley went by boat to Lerici, where he waited for a second boat that carried their furniture. Immediately he was ashore, he wrote to Mary in La Spezia.

[Lerici, Sunday, April 28th, 1822]

Dearest Mary,

I am this moment arrived at Lerici, where I am necessarily detained, waiting the furniture, which left Pisa last night at midnight; and as the sea has been calm, and the wind fair, I may expect them every moment. It would not do to leave affairs here in an *impiccio*, great as is my anxiety to see you. – How are you, my best love? How have you sustained the trials of the journey? Answer me this question, and how my little babe and C*** [Claire] are.

Now to business: – Is the Magni House taken? if not, pray occupy yourself instantly in finishing the affair, even if you are obliged to go to Sarzana, and send a messenger to me to tell me of your success. I, of course, cannot leave Lerici, to which place the boats (for we were obliged to take two) are directed. But you can come over in the same boat that brings this letter, and return in the evening.

I ought to say that I do not think that there is accommodation for you all at this inn; and that, even if there were, you would be better off at Spezzia; but if the Magni

House is taken, then there is no possible reason why you should not take a row over in the boat that will bring this – but don't keep the men long. I am anxious to hear from you on every account.

Ever yours,   S.

It may seem an odd thing, especially for a man who had already buried two children in Italy, that he should have his anxiety-ridden wife and two-year-old son on the move, furniture already shipped from under them, without knowing for certain whether they had a house to go to. In Shelley's case, it is what you'd expect. Williams, in his rather British way, conveys something of the chaos and unreadiness of their arrival.

Sunday, April 28th

Fine. Arrive at Lerici at 1 o'clock – the harbour-master called. Not a house to be had. On our telling him we had brought our furniture, his face lengthened considerably, for he informed us that the *dogana* would amount to £300 English, at least. Dined, and resolved on sending our things back without unlading – in fact, found ourselves in a devil of a mess.

If the local official was trying it on, he was let down by his haziness about rates of exchange. God knows what the harbour-master thought three hundred pounds sterling amounted to in local currency. Had he known that it was enough to rent a palazzo for about ten years, he would surely have adjusted his sights by an order of magnitude. When it came to the supposed customs duty on a parcel of furniture, he might have got thirty pounds without too much argument. As it was, his next superior seems to have seen that the job had been botched beyond repair.

Monday, 29th

Cloudy. Accompanied the harbour-master to the chief of the customs at Spezzia. Found him exceedingly polite, and willing to do all that lay in his power to assist us. He will, therefore, take on himself to allow the furniture to come on shore when the boats arrive, and then consider our house as a sort of depôt, until further leave from the Genoa government. Returned to Lerici somewhat calmed. Heard from Mary at Sarzana, that she had concluded for Casa Magni – but for ourselves no hope.

So there was just one house to go to. One house for all of them.

Our house, Casa Magni, was close to this village [San Terenzo]; the sea came up to the door, a steep hill sheltered it behind. The proprietor of the estate on which it was situated was insane; he had begun to erect a large house at the summit of the hill behind, but his malady prevented its being finished, and it was falling into ruin. He had (and this to the Italians had seemed a glaring symptom of very decided madness) rooted up the olives on the hillside, and planted forest trees. These were mostly young, but the plantation was more in English taste than I ever elsewhere saw in Italy . . . The scene was indeed of unimaginable beauty. The blue extent of the waters, the almost landlocked bay, the near castle of Lerici

. . . and distant Porto Venere . . . the tideless sea, leaving
no sands or shingle, formed a picture such as one sees in
Salvator Rosa's landscapes only.

This is Mary writing, and editing, some years later. The
reference to Salvator Rosa has a weight that is not immediately
obvious to a modern reader. Rosa was not just a landscape
painter: he was *the* landscape painter. He was the artist whose
work had been seized upon by architects and landscape-
makers like the Reptons around the turn of the century. The
medieval was in. The indispensable architectural style was a
revived Gothic, invoking a pre-rational age, when faith, fear
and mystery were the facts of life and all wisdom was ancient.
It is the architecture of overawing shadow – the famous
'Gothic gloom' – pierced by the fantastic dazzle of light
through stained glass.

Rich men, up with the latest tastes, who had read Richard
Payne-Knight's fashion-setting poem *The Landscape* – or had a
style adviser who had – now built houses to look like castles
rather than Greek temples. Not order and symmetry but
artful disorder and mystery were the things in garden and
landscape. If you could model the whole assembly of your
house and parkland along the lines of a landscape in a picture
of Salvator Rosa's, you had got it just about right. That is why
the movement was also known as 'The Picturesque'.

By invoking the work of Salvator Rosa, Mary lets us know
what kind of fashion lenses she was looking through. But
when she writes of this place as if it were the setting for an
idyll, she is not especially tinting those lenses. It is a place of
extraordinary beauty that, even today, feels detached from the

bustle of the world. It has not one but two castles to tease the Gothic imagination. The Genoese fortified the northern headland. Their Pisan rivals, in the days long-gone when Pisa was a power, outfaced them with the larger, more dramatic, fortress on the southern. Had she been a hippy, Mary would have told us about the vibes. Vibrations, indeed, seems to have been among the Shelleys' favourite words. But from the moment she moved into Casa Magni, Mary was picking up bad vibrations. The idea of a summer's idyll was what Edward Williams had carried in his mind when searching for houses to rent and for him, no doubt, parts of the next two months would turn out to be idyllic. For Jane, too, there would be certain nights and days of dreamy rapture. There would be not much rapture in it for Mary. At the beginning she would be sick, shrewish and angry and for as long as they stayed she was to be racked with a growing sense of foreboding that was not dissolved by the 'unimaginable' beauty of the bay.

> During the whole of our stay in Lerici, an intense presentiment of coming evil brooded over my mind, and covered this beautiful place and genial summer with the shadow of coming misery. I had vainly struggled with these emotions – they seemed accounted for by my illness.

Afterwards she would be widowed and sick with guilt. In between she nearly died. There were not to be many good days.

No one gave another thought to finding a separate house for the Williamses. When it came to it, they all piled into the Casa Magni. It was *force majeure* but there is nothing to suggest that the outcome was unwelcome as far as Shelley was concerned and obvious reasons to think it was exactly what he wanted. For Jane, *force majeure* gave her the close-up attention of not one but two devoted men in a private and – if you but looked out from the dilapidated house – beautiful world. They must have seemed to her two avatars of one ideal lover, they were so perfectly complementary: the soldier and the poet, the boot-and-saddle adventurer and the intellectual adventurer, each determined to adore her.

This fulfilling symmetry was possible because their relationship was beyond the dismal reach of bourgeois morality or the hypocrisies of guilt and fidelity. It was not the first time that Shelley had demonstrated his belief that a wife's love might be shared without diminution. In England he had done his best to persuade Mary to take his friend Thomas Hogg for a lover. Hogg was physically unappealing and Mary never overcame her reluctance, but she expressed no intellectual objections. She just asked for time. True love, she knew, was free love, free to turn, to move on, to embrace many, and not just one. She had to remember that these were the things said between them when the married Shelley, already father of a child, had come courting her. These were the justifications that had been in her mind that evening in the cemetery when she had given him her virginity somewhere in the region of her mother's grave. Jealousy was no more than the pernicious reciprocal of that pernicious institution, conventional marriage, that turned human love into slavery. The truly free lived beyond these things.

The Shelleys had spent the last year in Pisa much in the company of Edward and Jane Williams and Mary was well aware of Shelley's admiration for Jane. She knew better than to allow it to be a problem. After all, he was not long recovered from a spectacular seizure of infatuation with another improbably beautiful woman, Emilia Viviani, daughter of Pisa's governor. Her beauty had been no less improbable than her story, or, anyway, the story she managed to spin to the Shelleys. She had refused a suitor proposed by her parents. Their response was to have her enclosed against her will in the convent of Santa Anna until such time as she should submit to accept a suitor of their choosing. It was an emotional fantasy. The convent of Santa Anna was not a 'prison' but a boarding school – if, no doubt, one run on strict lines by nuns. Emilia's curiously Gothic tale was, in its way, an elaborated and much more imaginative version of the emotional blackmail that another unhappy schoolgirl, Harriet Westbrook, had used on Shelley ten years earlier. There had followed his first elopement, his first marriage. It had all ended – if it could be said to have ended at all, for Shelley was still living out the consequences – in disaster. The parallel should have occurred to him but that fatal appetite for emotional extremity had blinded him again. Emilia's implausible tale fired all that he had in him to burn.

In a state of emotional and poetic incandescence he had spent February writing what is, probably, the most uninhibited expression of sublime infatuation in the English language, *Epipsychidion*.

The title, a word which Shelley made up, will have seemed a little less opaque to the competent Greek scholars of Shelley's day than it does to the ordinary modern reader. It may be taken to mean 'song to the soul outside the self'. Its main idea is that Emilia cannot be another person that he happens to love but, in truth, must be another incarnation of his own soul to explain the depth of his love. He *is* Emilia; she *is* him.

It is an irresistible digression to mention that this poem – and especially this idea of merging selves – had a profound effect on at least one of its readers and so contributed to the making of the greatest of all Gothic novels. Indeed, there is no need to add the qualifying 'Gothic'. *Wuthering Heights* is among the greatest of all novels and it is the better understood for a reading of *Epipsychidion*. Emily Brontë, at fifteen, read and reread it with deliciously bated breath. It was addressed to her, after all. In the poem, Emilia is Englished into Emily.

> I never thought before my death to see
> Youth's vision thus made perfect. Emily,
> I love thee . . .
> > . . . Ah, me!
> I am not thine: I am a part of *thee*.

And here is Cathy, in the famous passage from *Wuthering Heights*, revealing to Nelly the deepest truth of her heart and mind on the day of Edgar Linton's proposal. She has accepted him. Was that wrong? The fact is, she loves Heathcliff, but it is love of altogether another order.

'If all else perished, and HE remained, I should still continue to be; and if all else remained, and he were annihilated, the universe would turn to a mighty stranger: I should not seem a part of it. – My love for Linton is like the foliage in the woods: time will change it, I'm well aware, as winter changes the trees. My love for Heathcliff resembles the eternal rocks beneath: a source of little visible delight, but necessary. Nelly, I AM Heathcliff! He's always, always in my mind: not as a pleasure, any more than I am always a pleasure to myself, but as my own being. So don't talk of our separation again: it is impracticable; and – '

The language, the images are all her own. She has plagiarised nothing but the thought. It is straight from *Epipsychidion*. Great writer that she is, she has expanded and deepened it into a psychological truth with genuine power to disturb. There is nothing swooning about Cathy's state. It could not be mistaken for infatuation. It is a far more profound and fatal, unalterable condition. Elsewhere in *Epipsychidion*, Shelley neatly summarises the tragedy at the core of *Wuthering Heights*:

> Ah, woe is me!
> What have I dared? Where am I lifted? How
> Shall I descend, and perish not?

Shelley, unlike Cathy and whatever Leigh Hunt may say about his being hard to please, was a serial swooner and Mary well knew it. More wearisome to her was that she was to bear most of the burden of housekeeping in a house that lay, as she now saw, several rocky miles of track from the nearest provisions. Just a month earlier she had found that she was pregnant once again. In her diary, she had marked it as 'a hateful day'. If there were to be moments when she found the tinkling of Jane's guitar a little less charming than her husband did, she might have been forgiven.

But then, for all that she was clever and imaginative, music was not among Mary's accomplishments and someone had to provide the music. Once, Claire had been the one who played and sang. She had done it sweetly enough to captivate Byron, however briefly:

> There be none of Beauty's daughters
> With a magic like thee;
> And like music on the waters
> Is thy sweet voice to me.
>
> . . .
>
> So the spirit bows before thee,
> To listen and adore thee;
> With a full but soft emotion,
> Like the swell of Summer's ocean.

Now there would be Jane, another of Beauty's daughters, around the house, casting her enviable music on the waters, but at least, as far as Mary was concerned, Jane wasn't Claire. In her own words, Mary's idea of bliss was the absence of Claire. It had taken a battle of wills with Shelley to get her out of their Pisa household and away to Florence, where she had lodged, reluctantly but respectably, as something between guest and governess. Yet, on the day they moved in, here she was with them once again, hurried out of Pisa and the neighbourhood of Lord Byron by Shelley because of the terrible news. News that she still had to be told.

As they waited for the cart to come bumping through the rain with their furniture, cleaning up a house that had been abandoned to the sea and the weather by a lunatic, it may not have seemed much of an idyll.

Three

Even the persuasive Ned Williams cannot make it sound like a promising start:

> *Wednesday, May 1st*
> Cloudy, with rain. Came to Casa Magni after breakfast; the Shelleys having contrived to give us rooms. Without them, heaven knows what we should have done. Employed all day putting the things away. All comfortably settled by four. Passed the evening in talking over our folly and our troubles.

'The style is the man,' said George-Louis LeClerc de Buffon, a man who probably thought his own name looked rather stylish when he wrote it down. (Style mattered to George-Louis, even when dead. There were fourteen liveried horses, sixty clerics and a choir of thirty-six in his cortège. The seventeen unstylish bladder stones found at autopsy were presumably left behind.) All the same, Buffon's rule faces something of a test when we look at the diary of Edward Williams. There is nothing here, not the faintest touch in his style, to hint at affinity with an infamously heterodox poet of genius who was, at times, unable to sort out his fantasies from reality. The style of the diary shows us a straightforward, slightly pompous, somewhat conceited man, whose evident enthusiasm does not save him from being just a little dull. For a bohemian, Williams has too sure a foot on his own social rung. He never gives a servant a name. Charles Vivian is always 'the servant' or 'the boy'. He believes he has aspirations to the life of the mind but, really, he is a hearty young man who lives in the world that lies to hand, sportingly occupied with the trim and tackle of things. If the style were altogether the man, it would take some imagination to see how this man became the friend in whose company Shelley took – in Mary's words – 'most delight' in the eighteen months between their meeting and their deaths, living at times in the same house and spending long days of this sultry summer in the same boat. There must have been more to him than he conveys with his pen.

There are some who believe that the answer is easy to see. In their reading, Williams's style is the result of his keeping, as it were, a straight bat. It is mentioned, as somehow suggestive evidence, that he and Shelley had been at Eton at the same time. Ancient Greece and Shelley's scholarly acquaintance with its customs, actual or supposed, are brought into the case. Shelley's lifelong tendency to fits of pain is put down, not to chronic inflammation of the kidneys – the likely cause – but to the psychological cramps of the closet. The dog-eared false syllogism is invoked: a great many men of extraordinary talent have been gay; Shelley was a man of extraordinary talent, ergo Shelley was gay. Ergo, the two men were gay lovers.

It won't do, though. As for Shelley, two elopements, three weddings, two wives, four children and a supposed seraglio, all by the age of twenty-four, is more heterosexual form that you can easily dismiss as a smoke-screen. In Williams's case there is nothing on file but modern suggestiveness. This is not to say that Williams was not enthralled by Shelley. It is clear that he was enthralled, just as it is clear that his company was all the more acceptable because it came in a parcel with the company of Jane with whom Shelley was, if not enthralled, certainly enamoured. It is both impossible and unnecessary to believe that Williams did not know it. While the two couples lived in separate apartments – but under the same roof – in Pisa, an uncomplicated man might just have declined to notice that Shelley was smitten with his wife, or that her response did not amount to a rebuff. In the hugger-mugger of life at Casa Magni he could not have been deluded. Besides, Shelley's notions of sexual love can have come as no surprise to either Edward or Jane Williams. It was from Shelley's cousin Medwin that Williams heard tales of the poet's extraordinary life and character. What he heard spurred him into the adventure of leaving Geneva and coming to Pisa with the object of joining Shelley's circle. The most circumspect account of Shelley's poetry and politics was bound to include some allusion to the poet's interesting sex-life and principles. It was hardly in Medwin's character to give a circumspect account of anything. He was a free-drinking cavalry officer, an insatiable party-goer and something of a cad into the bargain. The Williamses must have known what Shelley took no pains to hide and Medwin would certainly have advertised. In point of law, whether civil or ecclesiastical, it could be said that the Williamses were a more unorthodox couple than the Shelleys, who had, after all, taken marriage vows. The Williamses had taken none, as Jane was still the legal wife of a sea-captain she had unwisely married at sixteen and more wisely left at seventeen.

If their unsanctified relationship gave them a reason for

living out of England, money gave them another. A bank in India had collapsed and they had lost by it. Edward's half-pay stretched much more comfortably in a land where a palazzo of forty rooms could be rented for forty pounds a year and an apartment like theirs in Pisa for next to nothing. For the Williamses, Shelley's world was a foreign land within a foreign land and they had made their way there in haste, fully ready, it seems, to go native. Finding that Jane's beauty had captivated the poet was, surely, the perfect endorsement of their *entrée* into his world.

They were welcomed by the Shelleys, whose circle of acquaintance in Pisa had never been large. From the first they had recognised that the town was small and dull. It was, in Mary's words, 'a quiet, half unpeopled town'. But 'its very peace suited Shelley'. Its main virtue, for Mary, the now fretful mother of one surviving child, was the presence of an excellent doctor. (There is evidence that Professor Vacca was, in truth, the excellent doctor Mary thought him. Shelley consulted him about his bouts of pain and the general condition of his health, which was at least as unstable as any other hypochondriac's. Vacca told him that it would be best to give up consulting physicians, to stop taking medicine and to leave his complaint to Nature.)

In the winter, Pisa became somewhat less dull when the Tuscan court and its social machinery descended from Florence. As 1821 drew to a close, they got what they came for: the weather of early winter was fine and hot. With court and society came Byron to install himself in the imposing palazzo Lanfranchi, on the more fashionable northern Lungarno, with – the catalogue is Shelley's – 'ten horses, eight enormous dogs, three monkeys, five cats, an eagle, a crow and a falcon . . . five peacocks, two guinea hens, and an Egyptian crane . . . '

Edward and Jane did not come and go with the seasonal ebb and flow of the Tuscan court. They had been the Shelleys' companions all summer at Bagni di San Giuliano. For the winter each couple took an apartment in the same tall building, the Tre Palazzi della Chiesa, on the less fashionable southern Lungarno. It is clear that Edward and Jane were each bringing something to the party. The beautiful and musical Jane was by no means an intellectual but Edward was making efforts when it came to literature and there is no doubt that Shelley loved to play the role of teacher and leader in the world of the mind. Edward even took some German lessons from Claire and started to write a play. All the same, he was never going to provide a real intellectual gleam, any more than Jane was. But then, that was almost the whole point of their companionship. In June of 1821, Shelley writes to Claire: 'We see the Williamses constantly . . . nice, good-natured people. Very soft society after authors and pretenders to philosophy.'

What Edward really brought was his welcome talent and straightforward enthusiasm for practical doing. For practical doing aboard boats especially. During that first summer of their friendship, much time was spent sailing or drifting on the Serchio, on the Pisa canal or down the Arno to Livorno, with Williams always metaphorically on the quarterdeck. His qualifications may have been open to question on the day their brand-new little boat, carrying too much sail, was knocked flat, tipping them all into the Livorno canal. Still, we can be sure he would have had a confident and perfectly straightforward explanation for the problem. It would have been his style.

The straightforwardness that we see in Edward's diary may reflect a character that Shelley was, just then, most ready to find charming. A congenital weaver of cat's cradles himself, he had married a complicated woman from a tragi-comically complicated family and never taken a step with her that had not made her life and his more complicated. He had not lessened the complications by including the mercurial Claire in most of those steps and, with her, all the devious complications of her dealings with Byron. Where Byron was concerned, Shelley by now felt he'd seen enough of him for a lifetime – and it was not because his Lordship was too straightforward a character. Three weeks before his death, he wrote to Maria Gisborne, commenting on his retreat to so small a circle as that at Lerici: 'I detest all society – almost all, at least – and Lord Byron is the nucleus of all that is hateful and tiresome in it.' Shelley was more than ready to admit the possibility that Byron was, indeed, mad and bad. Edward Williams and Byron were opposite poles. For Shelley, the strongly magnetic Byron now repelled and, in accordance with the usual principle, the other pole was bound to attract.

Not the least attractive thing about the Williamses was the obvious warmth of the relationship between them. Shelley, on the other hand, had been out in the cold for some time. He admired Mary still but whether he still loved her was another matter. Mary still loved him, she knew that. She just could no longer show it. She had long since ceased to smile. Other kinds of warm response had become just as difficult for her. She had never shared the vivid and demonstrative character that so often exasperated her in Claire. Now, though, she had become, simply, cold. Mary, at twenty-four, had borne four children. The three she had conceived in England were all dead. The first had lived only days, unnamed. Clara, barely a year old, had died in their first year in Italy, dehydrated by an arduous journey that Shelley drove them to make in haste and in the worst heat of summer. She may never altogether have forgiven him for it, especially as the forced march – it amounted to that – all the way from Bagni di Lucca to Este had nothing to do with her own needs, everything to do with Claire's. (Byron had offered Shelley the use of his Este villa. What he didn't know was that Claire was there with him, still intent on reclaiming Allegra who was then in Venice. Shelley had lied, at least by ommission, in not mentioning the fact but, if Mary could only speed overland, they could all be there *en famille* before Byron found out. Claire could be passed off as newly arrived with Mary – they were sisters after all – and Byron could be merely displeased instead of apoplectic. It was just another of Shelley's cat's cradles but it cost the life of his daughter, sick even before the journey began.) After Clara's death, Mary fell into a depression from which she had not risen when William died, less than a year later, of malaria. She had spent that summer in Florence, pregnant again. Percy was now two and a half and she suffered spasms of frantic fear that he, too, would be taken away. Somewhere, deeply, she harboured a dread that these things were retribution for what she had done to Harriet. For the rest of her long life she would never be free of the notion that her hardships and trials were the penance demanded by fate. In 1822, the idea already weighed on her, as fatiguing as the Italian heat that Shelley loved and she did not. There were days of cold lashing rain, like the day when they moved in, but these were only punctuations in a long hot season of drought. Even when she wasn't pregnant, Mary found the heat exhausting. All in all, it is not hard to see that sex may have lost its rapture for Mary, or to understand why, in her own words, she had long since fallen into a way of 'involuntary freezing'.

Shelley was no less priapic than Byron but, despite all the public talk about his 'seraglio', he had never gone out of his way to create a public character built on his own erection as Byron had. Byron was the man who had begun his exile by arriving in Calais and falling immediately, 'like a thunderbolt', on the first chambermaid who came to hand. Byron, un-Byronically a most meticulous keeper of bills and ticker-off of accounts, was the man who recorded the fabulous cost in fees, gifts and incidental expenses of debauching a total of two hundred or more women in Venice. He was the man who recommended learning to make love the same way as you swim, which is to say, 'completely mechanically'. But if sex was for Byron a mechanical business, it was, as much as anything, the business of retribution, of putting up a score against womankind, mankind, lameness and the world. It was lucky, really, that Nature rewarded success on this shooting range with, at least, little spurts of pleasure. It was unlucky that she threw in booby prizes like the clap, a disease he caught like everybody else, and love, a disease he could only pretend to catch, with the possible exception of his deep feelings for Augusta, his half-sister. Apart from Augusta, in

Trelawny's words, 'he treated women as things devoid of soul or sense; he would not eat, pray, walk nor talk with them'.

Shelley, who felt and thought far otherwise, found Byron's attitudes revolting. His own special form of hypocrisy at least meant that he was more likely to catch a dose of love than the clap. He had, as Hunt said, defending him from calumny, no idea of sexual pleasure divorced from sentiment. If Byron's mistress, or for the short time that he was so provided, his wife, were not accommodating, Byron would bring home a whore or a star-struck girl. Shelley would never have done that. He might well, on the other hand, have brought home a woman he believed he truly loved. It is certain that he brought them home in his mind. The poetry is there to prove it. If Mary was cold and unreceptive, that first year in Pisa, there was Emilia Viviani for him to fantasise about. In the poem, the merely carnal is deliberately and explicitly put at a distance. The distance, it must be said, does not seem very great.

> To whatsoe'er of dull mortality
> Is mine, remain a vestal sister still;
> To the intense, the deep, the imperishable,
> Not mine but me, henceforth be thou united
> Even as a bride, delighting and delighted.

The climax of *Epipsychidion* is a vision of shared life on an Eden-isle of his imagining. If the isle is remote, the carnal is not.

> Our breath shall intermix, our bosoms bound,
> And our veins beat together; and our lips
> With other eloquence than words, eclipse
> The soul that burns between them, and the wells

Shelley's Boat

> Which boil under our being's inmost cells,
> The fountains of our deepest life, shall be
> Confused in Passion's golden purity,
> As mountain springs under the morning sun.

The poem ends with a fourfold ejaculation:

> I pant, I sink, I tremble, I expire!

It was Mary's customary task to make out the fair copies of Shelley's work and the sheets of *Epipsychidion* were passed to her just like everything else. If the suffused sexual excitement were no problem to her liberated mind ('Shelley's platonics', she calls them) it is hard to imagine she felt no pang reading,

> This isle and house are mine, and I have vowed
> Thee to be lady of the solitude.

They learned, inevitably, that La Viviani was not what their imaginations had made of her. Nobody could ever have been what Shelley's imagination had made of her but, all the same, the disillusion was both galling and shaming when she tried to screw money out of them. There was more than a little malice in Mary's saying that the conclusion of their friendship put her in mind of a 'nursery rhyme'.

> As I was going down Cranbourne Lane,
> Cranbourne Lane was dirty,
> And there I met a pretty maid,
> Who drop't to me a curtsey;
> I gave her cakes, I gave her wine,
> I gave her sugar candy,

Shelley's Boat

> But oh! The naughty little girl!
> She asked me for some brandy!

It is disingenuous in Mary to call this a 'nursery rhyme'. She well knows what kind of 'pretty maids' they were who dropped curtseys in dirty Cranbourne Lane behind St Martin's.

As an object of Shelley's idealised yearnings, Jane Williams was altogether more satisfactory. She, too, was beautiful. If she trailed no cloud of romantic plight, the fact that she was not locked up in a convent had obvious advantages. For a while, early in their acquaintance, Shelley had stopped visiting the Williamses in Pisa, telling them, in verse, that he could hardly bear the contrast between the warmth he found in their home and the coldness he found in his own. He feared, he says, that they would pity him. The hint is strong that, in the early months of this new and agreeable friendship, he did not trust himself to quell the expression of his impulses – and wanted them to know as much. The verses inspired by Emilia had gone straight to Mary for copying. Verses inspired by Jane, on the other hand, now go straight to Jane, with the instruction that they are not to be opened until she is alone. Or, significantly, with Williams. But not with Mary.

Now, a year on, Jane was out on the terrace, in the moonlight, singing. Or sometimes stroking his head on her lap to soothe away those unaccountable pains with her 'magnetic' healing. He had made his feelings clear. All the same, the lines he sent along with a lover's well-chosen – and suitably metaphor-laden – gift of a guitar, might have been written in the spirit of the *cavaliere servente*. (The guitar, by the by, now lies in the keeping of the Bodleian Library in Oxford. To know its catalogue number is such a melancholy thing that I shall not pass it on.) 'We Meet Not as We Parted', on the other hand, tells us that a moment had come when the last possible veil of ambiguity had certainly fallen off.

> We meet not as we parted,
> We feel more than all may see;
> My bosom is heavy-hearted,
> And thine full of doubt for me: –
> One moment has bound the free.
> That moment from time was singled
> As the first of a life of pain;
> The cup of its joy was mingled
> – Delusion too sweet though vain!
> Too sweet to be mine again.
>
> Sweet lips could my heart have hidden
> That its life was crushed by you,
> Ye would not have then forbidden
> The death which a heart so true
> Sought in your briny dew.

Whatever had, or had not quite, passed between them, it was the step that cannot be recalled. The transgression that cannot be sung or joked away. She had finally pushed him from her, it seems. But not that finally. Not for a moment did Jane – or Edward – show any sign of wishing to retreat from the intimacy of arrangements at Casa Magni. Only Mary would show signs – desperate signs by the end – of wanting to do that, but it was the place that she found hateful, not the arrangements.

Shelley's Boat

Mary was too much aware of her own estrangement from Shelley not to have been equally aware of this outbreak of the 'platonics'. But the fact is that later, both widowed, she and Jane would be, for a long time, fast friends. Mary refers to her sister-in-bereavement consistently as 'my darling Jane' or 'darling Janey'. She stresses their closeness and mutual affection to such a degree that, as with Shelley and Edward, a gay lobby has insisted on homosexual interpretations. The suggestion of a lesbian closeness between them, later on, is certainly not impossible to support. Mary was to cool only when Jane revealed that, after some local festival or other, she and Shelley had, indeed, made love. By the time of that confession, though, Mary was editing and publishing Shelley's works. She had become not merely the jealous guardian, but the tireless creator, of his remade reputation. Jane's sin, clearly, lay not so much in the act as in its disclosure at a time when Mary was busily rearranging the light in the shrine. You can't help feeling, either, that while Jane wanted the world to know that she and the poet had consummated the love that quivers through his verses to her, she was reducing a larger number of occasions to a more poetic and less scandalous unity. It was more hurtful, certainly, to Mary that Jane spoke to members of their London circle of her 'coldness' as a wife to Shelley. When she learned of it, though it cut deep, it was many months before she could bring herself to speak out and charge 'Janey' with betrayal. These things would bring an alteration but not an end to a relationship that Mary could not do without. I am running too far into their twined futures. Let us return to Casa Magni.

Four

Williams, in his journal, and true to his style, makes it seems as if the first week at San Terenzo was merely a little dismal owing to the weather.

Thursday, May 2d
Cloudy, with intervals of rain. Went out with Shelley in the boat – fish on the rocks – bad sport. Went in the evening after some wild ducks – saw nothing but sublime scenery, to which the grandeur of a storm greatly contributed.

Friday, May 3d
Fine. The captain of the port despatched a vessel for Shelley's boat. Went to Lerici with S., being obliged to market there; the servant having returned from Sarzana without being able to procure anything.

Saturday, May 4th
Fine. Went fishing with Shelley. No sport. Loitered away the whole day. In the evening tried the rocks again, and bad – no less than thirty baits taken off by the small fish. Returned late – a heavy swell getting up. I think if there are no tides in the Mediterranean, that there are strong currents, on which the moon, both at the full and at the change, has a very powerful effect; the swell this evening is evidently caused by her influence, for it is quite calm at sea.

Shelley's Boat

Sunday, May 5th

Fine. Kept awake the whole night by a heavy swell, which made a noise on the beach like the discharge of heavy artillery. Tried with Shelley to launch the small flat-bottomed boat through the surf; we succeeded in pushing it through, but shipped a sea on attempting to land. Walk to Lerici along the beach, by a winding path on the mountain's side. Delightful evening – the scenery most sublime.

Monday, May 6th

Fine. Some heavy drops of rain fell today, without a cloud being visible. Made a sketch of the western side of the bay. Read a little. Walked with Jane up the mountain.

After tea walking with Shelley on the terrace, and observing the effect of moonshine on the waters, he complained of being unusually nervous, and stopping short, he grasped me violently by the arm, and stared steadfastly on the white surf that broke upon the beach under our feet. Observing him sensibly affected, I demanded of him if he were in pain? But he only answered, by saying, 'There it is again – there!' He recovered after some time, and declared that he saw, as plainly as he then saw me, a naked child (the child of a friend who had lately died) rise from the sea, and clap its hands as in joy, smiling at him. This was a trance that it required some reasoning and philosophy entirely to awaken him from, so forcibly had the vision operated on his mind. Our conversation, which had been at first rather melancholy, led to this; and my confirming his sensations, by confessing that I had felt the same, gave greater activity to his ever-wandering and lively imagination.

The child of a friend who had lately died . . . This, of course, was the news that Shelley had been carrying with him, still suppressed, when they had moved in. Allegra had died. He had learned it from Byron on the 22nd of April. Typhus, always the camp-follower of famine, had flared all over Italy in the years after the war. The disease was on the wane, but it had found Allegra and taken not much more than a week to kill her. She was by then five and a quarter years old. Shelley had visited her at Bagnacavallo. She was very like Byron, he said. In Shelley's pocket or among his papers throughout all the upheaval was the letter from Byron.

April 23, 1822

. . . The blow was stunning and unexpected; for I thought the danger over, by the long interval between her stated amelioration and the arrival of the express. But I have borne up against it as I best can, and so far successfully, that I can go about the usual business of life with the same appearance of composure, and even greater. There is nothing to prevent your coming tomorrow; but, perhaps, today, and yester-evening, it was better not to have met. I do not know that I have anything to reproach in my conduct, and certainly nothing in my feelings and in-tentions towards the dead. But it is a moment when we are apt to think that, if this or that had been done, such event might have been prevented, though every day and hour shows us that they are the most natural and

inevitable. I suppose that Time will do his usual work –
Death has done his.

Yours ever, N.B.

Finding matter for reproach in his own conduct was
not one of Byron's talents, admittedly, but he might have
reflected on the fact that, in the time that Allegra had spent
with the nuns, he had not once paid her a visit. Still, he was
now to do his best by her. Even before he had written to
Shelley, he had written to his publisher, John Murray.

Pisa, April 22d 1822

Dear Sir, You will regret to hear that I have received intelli-
gence of the death of my daughter Allegra of a fever in the
Convent of Bagna Cavallo, where she was placed for the
last year, to commence her education. It is a heavy blow
for many reasons, but must be borne – with time.

It is my present intention to send her remains to England
for sepulture in Harrow Church (where I once hoped to
have laid my own), and this is my reason for troubling you
with this notice. I wish the funeral to be very private. The
body is embalmed, and in lead. It will be embarked from
Leghorn [Livorno]. Would you have any objection to give
the proper directions on its arrival?

I am yours, etc., N.B.

You are aware that protestants are not allowed holy ground
in catholic countries.

In a Protestant country, they were fastidious in other ways.
The Rector of Harrow Church, near Peachey Stone where the
poet had spent so many hours as a boy, refused to inter the

illegitimate corpse as and where Byron proposed. He allowed her to be buried just inside the threshold of the church. Aristocracy has some sway, after all: even that grudging 'just inside' is a concession that no plain Mister was likely to win. Byron had wanted a memorial with the words: 'I shall go to her, but she shall not return to me.' The Rector allowed no memorial. Allegra was later reburied, still unmarked, in a corner of the churchyard and for a few years her grave was discernible as a hump. It settled and all trace vanished.

It was all over and done with, arrangements made, the child embalmed and wrapped in lead, the freight in hand, her resting place decided and, still, no one had told Allegra's mother. She had been a few streets away in Pisa, newly arrived in Shelley's house from Florence, even as Byron was writing the news to Shelley, but on that rainy, blustery 1st of May at Casa Magni she still did not know. 'Employed all day putting the things away. All comfortably settled by four. Passed the evening in talking over our folly and our troubles.' Williams is almost never revealing except unconsciously and between the lines. It may sometimes be discretion but you can't help but feel there were things that the straightforward Mr Williams didn't take on board. Women's things.

The evening when they discussed their folly and troubles was the evening that Shelley told her. Claire walked into the room unexpectedly to hear somebody mention Bagnacavallo. The silence that followed told her almost as much as words were going to.

She took it with a peculiar frozen calm. Later came tears, floods of tears, but no hysterics, no rage, not the violent reaction Shelley had feared and expected of the always volatile, impulsive Claire.

It is not likely that either Shelley or Mary would have offered her the platitude, 'Life goes on.'

Still, beyond the platitude there was the fact and no one knew it better or more bitterly than Mary. She had lost three babies. She was now, as Claire must have known, pregnant again and vomiting daily. For Claire, though, it wasn't going to be like that and she seems to have known it by deep instinct. If the affair with Byron had moulded her life, the death of Allegra somehow froze its shape for ever. She was to live a long life and not an easy one, earning her frugal living as governess and companion, never to marry and never to have another child. In her own exquisite phrase, it was to be hers to 'study how to be happy without happiness'. She seems to have known it from that 1st of May. She was twenty-four when they broke the news. She had been twenty-three when Allegra died. Her twenty-fourth birthday had fallen in the hectic week or so between. It may not have gone altogether unremarked, if only because of the coincidence that April 27th was also Edward Williams's birthday. He had just reached twenty-nine. Some time earlier, in Pisa, his journal tells us that he had 'begun a drama'. Had there been much of the dramatist in Ned Williams, he might have found room in his journal for noting something besides the 'poor fishing' that seems to sum up his week.

Five

Byron had left England in 1816 and had not been short of reasons for going. For one thing, he had enormous debts and bailiffs were camped out in his Piccadilly mansion, on which he had not paid and could not pay the year's rent. The big reason, though, was the scandal of his wife's flight from him after barely a year of marriage. In fact, Annabella did not tell him she was leaving until after she had gone and, even then, never told him why she had gone. Her reasons were not disclosed in the action for separation. There was no legal reason that they should have been disclosed but the fact only confirmed the common knowledge of the town: they were simply too shocking to be made public. In what way they were shocking was left to the world's imagination and, therefore, every imaginable shocking thing was believed to be the case.

Her desertion left a wound that never ceased to fester. 'The moral Clytemnestra of thy Lord', he called her, casting himself – with a mixture of vanity and prophecy – as Greek hero. (Agamemnon may have led the Greeks against Troy but, like most husbands, he failed to be a hero to his wife, Clytemnestra. She killed him.) Annabella had not killed Byron, but he had certainly looked for his analogy in the right place. The family life of the Gordons had, for generations, been much like family life in the *Oresteia*. Violence, incest, madness and all.

Shelley, leaving England two years later, had an even

lumpier stew of reasons for following Byron to the Dover packet. He, too, faced scandal concerning his marriage. In his case, marriages. When Shelley and Mary eloped it was an entirely new experience for her but not for him. In the case of Harriet Westbrook, mind you, the elopement part seems to have been arranged only for the sake of adventure, as Harriet's father, a coffee-house keeper, made no objection to his daughter's marrying a baronet's son with expectations. Shelley may never have been quite convinced that he loved Harriet, but his heart had been reached because she found her school a kind of hateful captivity. This was a feeling Shelley understood. Harriet got it across that Shelley or suicide were her only choices and so he ran away with her to Scotland where they were married in August of 1812, just four days after Shelley's twentieth birthday. Harriet was sixteen. A child soon came. Even sooner came the inevitable recognition, on Shelley's part, of the distance between them in mind and character.

Then, eighteen months or so after marrying Harriet, he met Mary Godwin. This time, no question, it was love. If he was an apostle of freedom, the beautiful Mary was freedom's daughter. Her mother – who had died after giving birth to her – had been Mary Wollstonecraft, the pioneer of women's rights. Her father – a man who had confessed himself 'unequal to the education of daughters' but felt no such inhibition about educating the entire world – was William Godwin, the revolutionary author of *Political Justice*, a work of great influence with the angry young men of the day. Godwin's philosophy regarded conventions like marriage, family, law, government and so on as pernicious institutional bric-à-brac, impediments to human happiness to be swept away by revolution. These, of course, are the ancestor ideas of the hippie 'revolution'. John Lennon's 'Imagine' might be a kind of post-it-note version of Godwin's more compendious thesis. Godwin's arguments are more rigorous and impressive than Lennon's simple and wishful lyrics but the same fatal, fatuous flaw is there in both. They are untainted by any reference to human experience. In fact, Godwin had been steadily unpicking his own work. In later editions he had rescinded or diluted much of the stuff that Shelley had taken neat. Shelley had taken Godwin's teaching straight from the unadulterated first edition, and he had taken it to heart. It was, therefore, clear to him that such a heart had the right to fly where the soul led and a worn-out marriage should be no impediment. By Godwin's own principles, he believed he had every right to make love to Godwin's daughter.

Less than a month after he had met Mary and been truly smitten, he took the unlikely step of marrying Harriet again. This time in London. This may seem an irrational thing for any man to have done, especially a rationalist who did not believe in marriage. There was a prosaic reason. By a marriage under English law, Shelley made sure that there would be no doubt as to the legitimacy of Harriet's child – or, as it was about to turn out, children – or their claims on his estate. This was not a case of Shelley, in his paradoxical way, trying to do the decent thing before leaving. It was the money lenders who insisted. A post-obit bond was a way to raise present money on the strength of future inheritance. The cash you got was much discounted compared to what the lender would collect when death brought settlement day around. If the borrower were to die before coming into his expectation, the debt and its liabilities simply passed, like the expected inheritance, to his own heirs. To his legitimate heirs, that is. In this regard, jiggery-pokery Scottish marriages between runaway minors did not offer the copper-bottomed certainty that money-lenders look for. Whether Shelley explained it in quite these terms to Harriet is doubtful, but she may have been persuaded that it was in her own legal interests. Still, it is not all that odd that she got it into her head that going to church and getting married – again – meant something like a rapprochement, so it is understandable that at or about the time of this second wedding, she conceived their second child. It is even more understandable that she was confused and distressed when Shelley got round to explaining that the wedding made no difference. He was leaving her for Mary. Five months later, as Harriet's belly was swelling, Shelley eloped with Mary, not quite seventeen, from Godwin's house. They ran away to France.

With them went Mary's stepsister, Mary Jane, soon to start calling herself Claire and then just turned sixteen. Even for Shelley, it was something of a triumph of unorthodoxy to elope with an extra woman. It may have seemed to them that Mary Jane's presence gave the party some faint appearance of respectability. In fact, the reverse was more often the case. It seems to have been true that Claire spoke French with more fluency than Shelley but it would have been inconceivably modest of him to feel that he could not get by without her help. He did, after all, read French literature quite happily. The answer probably lies in the characters of the two girls. Radical in thought and imagination as she may have been,

Shelley's Boat

Mary was not a creature of impulse and high excitement. That is exactly what Claire was. When it came to the reality of creeping from the house in the pale dawn it suddenly seemed an enormous thing to do. They left. They scuttled back. Then they left again and it was done. It perfectly expressed the characters of the two girls. The equivocation and retreat were Mary's. The urge to get on with the adventure, Claire's. Shelley understood the chemistry. If both were in on it, they would probably make the rendez-vous at his street corner where he had a carriage waiting. If just Mary, he'd have been much less certain that she'd turn up. As to the rest, the sheer awkwardness of a honeymoon-plus-one, it's easy to believe that they simply did not think it out. After all, the girls did not take a change of clothes, even though the adventure, for a while at least, would involve the idea of walking to Switzerland. Eloping is the business of leaving the note, leaving the house and getting to the Dover Road. The rest is just mileage. It took the two of them to take those first steps but, if Mary had realised quite how much of the mileage of her married life Claire would be tagging along for, her screams would have woken everybody in Skinner Street.

Harriet bore Shelley a son in November of 1814, by which time Mary in turn was swelling up, five months pregnant, with a daughter. Two years later, to the month, Harriet left her lodgings and did not return. Her body was found in the Serpentine a few days later. She was, again, according to *The Times*, in 'advanced pregnancy'. Shelley, this time, had nothing to do with her pregnancy. The same could hardly be said of her suicide. She had taken up with a military officer.

If he gave her any assurances on the way to enjoying her, they were hollow. For the second time in her life she found herself abandoned by a man who had just taken the trouble to impregnate her. She was twenty years old.

It wasn't the first suicide to hit Shelley and Mary with shock and guilt as that winter began. In October 1816, Mary's half-sister, Fanny Imlay, killed herself with an overdose of laudanum while staying at an inn where no one knew her in Swansea. She and Mary had both, perhaps, inherited depressive tendencies from their mother, who had made two attempts at suicide. The first time, she had tried laudanum. The second time, she had taken a leap from Putney Bridge. Of the three girls in Godwin's house, it was Fanny – the one with no remaining natural parent – who had long been the natural outsider. When Shelley came, she was as much smitten as any of them but she was the outsider still. When the great moment of the elopement had come, Claire had been included and she had been excluded, with whatever was in her heart left unconsidered. How unbearable that had been was now clear enough. The Godwins responded to her death with what seems shocking inhumanity, anxious to avoid the scandal of what was, then, a criminal act. She had considered this, and them. She had died with nothing about her to connect them to her. They left things that way. She was buried where she had died, far from home, anonymous, in a pauper's grave. By way of epitaph, she has the scant six lines in which Shelley recalled – or, rather, found that he could not altogether recall – the last time he had seen her.

Shelley's Boat

On Fanny Godwin

Her voice did quiver as we parted,
Yet knew I not that heart was broken
From which it came, and I departed
Heeding not the words then spoken.
Misery – O misery,
This world is all too wide for thee.

So far, all that is scandalous and blameable about the Shelleys' history had not circulated much beyond their own acquaintance, their Marlow neighbours – the gentry shunned them – and certain literary circles. That changed when Harriet's family fought Shelley at law over the two surviving children. A bare three weeks after Harriet's death, Shelley and Mary were married. Their lawyer said it would help his case. He was wrong, as half the lawyers in every case always, and expensively, will be. In the High Court of Chancery, Lord Chancellor Eldon decided that Shelley was unfit to have the custody of his own children. Extracts from Shelley's *Queen Mab: A Philosophical Poem*, printed and circulated privately in a small edition in 1813, were quoted to show that he was an immoral atheist who believed in free love. He was also a vegetarian, which didn't go down well, either.

Trelawny's summing up is surely as succinct as any that Lord Eldon could have managed, though Eldon might not have appreciated his savage irony.

It must not be forgotten, that Shelley lived in the good old times, under the paternal government of the Tories, when liberal opinions were prohibited and adjudged as contraband of war. England was then very much what Naples is now.

Sidney Smith is of one mind with Trelawny.

From the beginning of the century to the death of Lord Liverpool was an awful period for anyone who ventured to maintain liberal opinions. He was sure to be assailed with all the Billingsgate of the French Revolution; 'Jacobin', 'Leveller', 'Atheist, 'Incendiary', 'Regicide', were the gentlest terms used, and any man who breathed a syllable against the senseless bigotry of the two Georges was shunned as unfit for social life.

Shelley had breathed more than a syllable or two but he hadn't breathed them to nearly as many people as he would have wished. When the extracts from *Queen Mab* were read out in court, one wonders whose copy the prosecution was using. The twenty-one-year-old Shelley had published the poem in 1813 and on the title page he is named as both author and printer. Only about seventy copies saw the light of day, privately distributed. It was the philosophical notes that he added to the text that furnished such rich pickings for the prosecution. They amounted to a digest of Godwin's revolutionary political economy, leavened with extensive quotations from Rousseau, whose name, to Lord Chancellor Eldon, would have been French for Beelzebub. A random selection is enough to mark out Shelley's political ground clearly enough:

There is no real wealth but the labour of man. Were the

mountains of gold and the valleys of silver, the world would not be one grain of corn the richer; no one comfort would be added to the human race.

*   *   *

The poor are set to labour – for what? Not the food for which they famish: not the blankets for want of which their babes are frozen by the cold of their miserable hovels: not those comforts of civilisation without which civilised man is far more miserable than the meanest savage . . . No; for the pride of power, for the miserable isolation of pride, for the false pleasure of the hundredth part of society. No greater evidence is afforded of the wide extended and radical mistake of civilised man than this fact: those arts which are essential to his very being are held in the greatest contempt; employments are lucrative in inverse ration to their usefulness: the jeweller, the toy-man, the actor gains fame and wealth by the exercise of his useless and ridiculous art; whilst the cultivator of the earth, he without whom society must cease to subsist, struggles through contempt and penury, and perishes by that famine which, but for his unceasing exertions would annihilate the rest of mankind.

*   *   *

English reformers exclaim against sinecures, – but the true pension list is the rent-roll of the landed proprietors: wealth is a power usurped by the few, to compel the many to labour for their benefit. The laws which support this system derive their force from the ignorance and credulity of its victims: they are the result of the conspiracy of the few against the many . . .

* * *

Love is free: to promise for ever to love the same woman is not less absurd than to promise to believe the same creed: such a vow, in both cases, excludes us from all inquiry.

* * *

A system could not well have been devised more studiously hostile to human happiness than marriage.

* * *

In fact religion and morality, as they now stand, compose a practical code of misery and servitude: the genius of human happiness must tear every leaf from the accursed book of God ere man can read the inscription on his heart.

* * *

Lord Bacon says that atheism leaves to man reason, philosophy, natural piety, laws, reputation, and everything that can serve to conduct him to virtue; that superstition destroys all these, and erects itself into a tyranny over the understandings of men: hence atheism never disturbs the government, but renders man more clear-sighted, since he sees nothing beyond the boundaries of the present life.

* * *

The quotations from Rousseau – untranslated – amount to several pages of the published text of *Queen Mab*, and lead to a pair of questions concerning God that had infuriated Popes, princes and parish priests all over Europe: 'S'il est inconcevable, pourquoi nous en occuper? S'il a parlé, pourquoi l'univers n'est-il pas convaincu?'

The footnotes alone were enough to scupper Shelley's hopes. The children were made wards of court and put into guardianship. Better for these children, said the Lord Chancellor, that they should be made orphans than be handed back to such a father. What right of access he was granted came with severe limitations: it was ordered that he should never be in the children's company except in the presence of their guardians. To rub it in, the Westbrooks, his social inferiors by a gulf, were granted unlimited access without conditions. It amounted to his being judged mad and bad. In Byron's case that had been the private opinion of Lady Lamb, who was herself completely barmy. In Shelley's case it had the force of law. It outraged him but it frightened him, too.

Leigh Hunt believed that Shelley's ill reputation in England could be put down to the effect of the Lord Chancellor's judgment. After Shelley's death, he would be at pains to remove what remained of the tar and feathers:

He was said to be keeping a seraglio at Marlow, and his friends partook of the scandal. This keeper of a seraglio, who, in fact, was extremely difficult to please in such matters, and who had no idea of love unconnected with sentiment, passed his days like a hermit. He rose early in the morning, walked and read before breakfast, took that meal sparingly, wrote and studied the greater part of the morning, walked and read again, dined on vegetables (for he took neither meat nor wine), conversed with his friends (to whom his house was ever open), again walked out, and usually finished with reading to his wife till ten o'clock, when he went to bed. This was his daily existence. His book was generally Plato, or Homer, or one of the Greek tragedies, or the Bible, in which last he took a great, though peculiar, and often admiring interest.

It reads a little too much like an extract from *Lives of the Saints*, but then the impoverished Hunt had always been the object of Shelley's generosity. The coin of personal loyalty was all he had to be generous with in return but, at the time of Eldon's judgment, there weren't many in England who would have chosen to believe Hunt's picture. For the government it was more useful, and for most other people simply more fun, to paint the poet in the lurid colours of depravity. The editors of today's tabloids would not miss the chance to splash Lord Chancellor Eldon's judgment against a minor celebrity. Their moral ancestors were no different and anything tending to destroy Shelley's character, moreover, would have had the encouragement of the political establishment.

Shelley began to worry more and more that his other children – Mary's children – would be taken from him, too, and an old fear from his childhood was revived: that his father would try to have him confined for insanity. This had started off as a servant's joke but it was true that a state of complete and hostile estrangement had long existed between father and son. The idea that his father would call him mad was certainly not a mad idea. The idea that a court would agree with him and make the necessary order may have taken a little more imagination, but not so much as to make his fear ridiculous. Not now.

Shelley's conviction that the authorities kept watch on him was probably not a delusion, either. Maybe a government snooper had once taken pot-shots at him, as he believed, or maybe not, but there's little doubt that he was watched and followed. Somewhere or other, there was a dossier with his name on it. It will have contained some note of his having been sent down from Oxford for sending a pamphlet, written by himself and his undergraduate friend, a youth with the somewhat telling name of Thomas Jefferson Hogg, to the heads of all the colleges and all the bishops of the Church of England. Its title was *The Necessity of Atheism* and it went down as well as might be expected in an institution where holy orders were a necessary qualification for a college fellowship. Going to Ireland, after his expulsion, to lend his voice to political agitation, must have added a chapter. Falling under the spell of Godwin will have contributed more than a footnote. The authorities had, certainly, considered a prosecution against Godwin for the publication of *Political Justice*. Now and again, though, even in the gloom of Whitehall, there are flashes of common sense. A copy of *Political Justice* did not come cheap and somebody had been wise enough to conclude that no book costing three guineas could circulate widely enough to do as much harm as publicising it in court would do.

If the government was fearful and watchful it was because it had every reason to be. The third King George was drivelling through his long, insane senility. The fat man waiting impatiently to be the fourth King George presented his many hungry and discontented future subjects with the most impressive embodiment of vanity and conspicuous consumption since Henry VIII. The Prince of Wales, like Henry, was a serial adulterer and a bigamist but he lacked the tyrant's power to quell the tide of brilliant, and often spectacularly obscene, satire that pointed up these flaws for the amusement and education of the public. But the comic froth of squibs and lampoons swirled on the surface of a much deeper brew of thoroughgoing political unrest.

Waterloo may have ended the war but it had not brought peace to England. The class war was as hot as at any time in her history. Seventeen Luddites were hanged in York in 1815, but it did not stop the machine-breaking. The Corn Laws, forbidding the import of corn until the price of the home-grown item had reached a peak of cruelty, were introduced that same year. They seemed good laws to landowners, who had votes, but less good to the millions going hungry, who didn't. There was a widespread, angry appetite not just for bread but for change. The now unwanted soldiery who had been shipped home and turned into the streets were an uncomfortable presence in every town and city. The mutilated begged, while those who were whole roamed in search of work they had little chance of finding. The Cato Street Conspiracy – a kind of back-street plan to tool up, go forth and kill the entire cabinet – and the Peterloo Massacre were the kind of trouble that was brewing.

It was but four years since the Prime Minister had been shot down in the lobby of the House of Commons. Improbably enough, the man with the gun had no political motive. He had suffered reverses in business, believed the government had denied him compensation that he was owed and seemed to think of assassination as a form of appeal procedure. However insane his motives, his action carried a political warning. There were many reasons for the fretful surveillance of self-proclaimed revolutionaries like Shelley.

Among all the reasons for leaving England there was another that pointed directly to Italy. There was Claire's baby. Byron had acknowledged that Alba, as she was at first to be called, was his child while she was still in the womb. It was time to yield her up to his keeping, in accordance with their agreement, and Byron was in Venice. How long he might stay in Venice depended on his unpredictable whim. Mary, therefore, was eager to see the contract closed. Were Byron to move on to God-knows-where, she could see that Claire and her baby might be wished on them for ever.

Then there were the families. When Shelley's grandfather died it had taken months to settle the business of his inheritance. When the wrangling was over, Shelley was much better off but relations with his father were no more cordial.

It was not lost on him that Godwin, who had at one time cut him in the street and refused to deal with him except through lawyers, softened towards him now he had come into money. In fact, Godwin now began to sponge on Shelley, and was to keep it up for the rest of his life, borrowing huge sums with a knack for being abusive even as he held out his hand for more.

Then there was Shelley's health. He had once been told, and believed, that he was dying of consumption. The symptoms had all disappeared but Shelley's tendency to hypochondria had not. For a time he was convinced that he had elephantiasis. He did suffer – and to the end of his life would suffer – from regular fits of nephritis, causing crippling pain. All these things, he was advised, would be the better for living in a warmer, drier climate.

This advice brings us to one further and greater reason for leaving England, one greater and more overwhelming cause of national and personal discontent. It was one over which neither politician nor physician had the slightest power. It was the bloody weather.

Six

At the best of times, we who live in northern Europe feel the longing that Keats felt for the warm south, or Goethe for 'das Land, wo die Zitronen blühn'. They may have yearned the more strongly because the teens of the nineteenth century were not the best of times. Not by a long way.

In fact, the world's weather had fallen sick. In Europe and North America, 1816 was called 'the year without a summer'. No doubt the phrase had its equivalent in all the other languages of the northern hemisphere. Snow fell at midsummer in New England. Eskimos journeyed as far south as the coasts of England. Those crops not killed by deep, late frosts were stunted for want of sun or blighted by the moulds and mildews that thrived in the dim, incessantly rainy months that should have been summer. There was famine in Ireland, as there would be again thirty years later, but in 1816 the Irish were not a special case. The great hunger extended all the way to China with its familiar companions, typhus and cholera. Millions died.

It was the year that Byron wrote his poem 'Darkness':

I had a dream, which was not all a dream.
The bright sun was extinguish'd, and the stars
Did wander darkling in the eternal space,
Rayless, and pathless, and the icy earth
Swung blind and blackening in the moonless air;

Morn came and went – and came, and brought no day,
And men forgot their passions in the dread
Of this their desolation; and all hearts
Were chill'd into a selfish prayer for light.

It was the year, too, of the famous gathering at Villa Diodati, on the shores of Lake Geneva, when, as a way of passing the time indoors, the weather being so rotten, Byron suggested a competition to see who could come up with the best tale about things ghostly and macabre. Byron's personal physician, Polidori, produced and later published *The Vampyre*, working up a discarded suggestion of Byron's and laying the foundation not so much of a literary genre as of a whole entertainment industry. (When first published it was thought to be by Byron himself. For what it's worth, Goethe thought it was the best thing he'd written.) Given that both Byron and Shelley – each too chary of being outdone – had slacked out of the competition altogether, you would think Polidori's *Vampyre* would have been the outright winner. Of course, he finished a distant second to Mary Shelley's entry, *Frankenstein*, which did not so much found a literary genre as a whole new way of thinking about what it is to be human. It is not coincidental that her story begins and ends in a wintry, ice-bound world.

What was it that had darkened the skies and chilled the world? There was not one cause but several, hideously coinciding. The biggest was a volcanic explosion on the island of Sambawa, east of Bali. Mount Tambora used to be about four thousand metres in height. Since the 11th of April 1815 it has been twelve hundred metres shorter and what is left is hollowed into a huge crater. It was the greatest volcanic explosion since the earliest records of human history and one hundred and fifty times more powerful than the 1980 explosion of Mount St Helens in the United States. The sound was heard nearly a thousand miles away. It takes only two weeks for the stratospheric plume of a great eruption to girdle the earth. It takes years for it all to come down again. As it does, it leaves its mark as a dust layer, preserved in the ice sheets of Greenland. Examinations of core samples confirm the historical reports of the magnitude of Tambora's explosion. What they also show is that in 1808 or 1809 there had been another eruption almost as great as Tambora's. What mountain went up and where it was, nobody knows. Astonishingly enough, only two centuries ago, the beaten tracks of mankind left enough of the world untouched for such a thing to pass without report.

Even before Tambora, then, the world was being cooled by a screen of volcanic debris. Between these two great events, there were other, smaller but significant eruptions in the Caribbean. What darkened the skies and quenched the sun was sulphurous ash, whole mountains of it. But even all of this was not the only cause of a cooling world and unpredictable weather.

There may be no point in remarking that what heats the world is the sun. There may, on the other hand, be some point in remembering that warming the earth is not the point of the sun's existence. The sun goes about its own business. It just so happens that fluctuations in its business cycle result in fluctuations in the earth's temperature.

There is the well-known, approximately eleven-year-long,

cycle in the occurrence of sunspots, those visible whirlpools in the sun's magnetic fields. Sunspots are associated with variations in the amount of energy the sun radiates. Times when there are few sunspots are cooler than times of many. The effect is small but measurable in its effects on earth over the eleven-year cycle. There are much longer cycles and, sometimes, long periods of apparent anomaly in the sun's magnetic activities. These both seem to have a greater influence on earthly weather. From 1645 to 1715, for instance, the sun seems to have been magnetically remarkably lazy. There was no shortage of reliable astronomers observing the sun in the second half of the seventeenth century, and they were seeing few or no sun-spots. The nineteenth-century German astronomer Gustav Spörer pulled together observations made between 1672 and 1699 and found fewer than fifty sunspots recorded. To get an idea of how different this is, you only have to know that in a typical thirty-year period of the twentieth century somewhere between forty thousand and fifty thousand spots are likely to have been reported. During the seventy years that this period of minimal solar activity lasted, the weather was terrible. Longer and colder winters were separated by colder, less reliable summers. The growing season in Europe was consistently shortened by one or sometimes two months. The result was chronic shortages punctuated by famines, accompanied by visitations of all the diseases that afflict humanity in such conditions. The period of this solar doze is known to astronomers as the 'Maunder Minimum'. Another sustained period of magnetic laziness in the sun – the 'Dalton Minimum' – was recorded between 1795 and the 1820s, coincidentally and almost perfectly matching the years of Shelley's life. It, too, was responsible for a colder, less predictable climate and, by the by, made 1812 a bad year to pick for invading Russia. When Mount Tambora threw its vast mass into the equation, producing even greater effects on the weather than the magnetic quiescence of the sun, it was acutely worsening a climate that was already suffering.

A digression is irresistible. Antonio Stradivari timed his birth well. He was born in 1644 and thus lived and worked through the Maunder Minimum. More to the point, so did the Alpine spruce that he used in making his violins. Cold winters and cool summers mean slow growth, especially so in the north-slope wood that luthiers prefer in their search for tone-woods. A long run of such conditions means growth that is not only slow but also even over the whole life of the tree. The annual rings are close and, from ring to ring, the amount of weak, fast produced, early-season wood is at a minimum compared to strong, late-season wood. The result is spruce with ideal qualities of strength and resonance. The secret of Stradivari and his great contemporaries has nothing to do with mysterious lost recipes for varnish but much to do with the mysterious life of the sun.

Stradivari made more than eleven hundred instruments, so cherished that more than six hundred are still with us. The most illustrious, called 'The Messiah', was made in 1716, at the end of this long phase. It would be interesting to know whether musicians are aware of any special quality in violins made of spruce that grew up, along with Shelley, through the Dalton Minimum. Allowing for seasoning of the timber, that would probably mean violins from good makers around 1830. Please let me know.

Whatever the effect might be on musical tone-woods, the compounding of serial volcanic explosions of barely imaginable magnitude with the effects of a long downturn in the solar economy is a sure recipe for rotten weather, and lots of it. When Shelley went to Italy, the screen of dust was thinning and the sun had begun to turn the magnetic corner. Weather in the northern hemisphere, in short, had started to look up. For us children of the north, the hot, bright days and velvet nights of Italy still exercise their seduction. We like the change and we are ready to pay for it. For Shelley's generation it was beyond change. It was a transformation more like alchemy, changing much of life's lead into gold.

For the painter Turner, arriving in Italy a year after Shelley, it's not too much to say the effect was not dissimilar to taking LSD. It had a profound effect on his relations with light and colour. Over two months he made something like twenty-five colour sketches a day, leading to the masterpieces of *San Giorgio Maggiore* and *Looking East from the Giudecca*. The fantastic sunsets that he blazed into paint and that find their way into Shelley's poetry were also products of Tambora's ashes, still in the sky. One of the few unarguably appealing things about Casa Magni was the broad terrace, perched on its strange arcade above the beating waves and offering its vast view to the west. Tambora must still have painted a sunset or two for Shelley.

Seven

She came into their lives on a Sunday afternoon. The weather was cloudy and threatening but they didn't let that dim the excitement of her arrival or the eagerness of their welcome.

Sunday, May 12th 1822
Mr. Maglian, (harbour-master at Lerici), called after dinner, and while walking with him on the terrace, we discovered a strange sail coming round the point of Porto Venere, which proved at length to be Shelley's boat. She had left Genoa on Thursday, but had been driven back by prevailing bad winds. A Mr. Heslop, and two English seamen brought her round, and they speak most highly of her performances. She does, indeed, excite my surprise and admiration. Shelley and I walked to Lerici, and made a stretch off the land to try her, and I find she fetches whatever she looks at. In short, we have now a perfect plaything for the summer.

Journal of Edward Elleker Williams

She was a schooner. Or perhaps a ketch. Or in at least one picture a yawl but that has to be wrong. Or a cutter. Trelawny, who ought to know, calls her a schooner but then he also says she is 'Torbay-rigged', and a definition of Torbay rig is hard to come by. To most of the world, a boat by any other name is just a sailor's trick to wrong-foot the landlubber. To others – many, many others – to bookish sleuths, nit-picking

74

enthusiasts, warring biographers and a great web of midnight computer-clickers, this sort of thing matters. There has been much sword-swishing over the literary salvage value of this tiny, verbal piece of the wreckage. It's no use arguing that words and the way we use them are liable to a certain amount of slop and altering in the wash. When Shelley referred to 'Anarchy', for instance, he meant something quite different from what a modern reader takes that word to mean. This matters a little, as Shelley wrote poems about 'Anarchy', but whether the vessel he sat in, on that last afternoon of his life, was a schooner or a ketch can't really be said to alter much.

Still, it seems you have to take a position on this question and so it must be looked into. Shelley's boat, thirty feet long or so, undecked and having two masts, was built in Genoa to a design provided by the customer. Her lines were based, according to what Mary tells us, on 'a model taken from one of the Royal Dockyards', but one that had been discovered to have some fatal flaw. 'I have since heard,' she says, 'that there was a defect in this model, and that it was never seaworthy.' The suggestion that the design of Shelley's boat might some-how be traced back to the Admiralty is, surely, an unmerited slander on their Lordships' competence. Williams, as Trelawny says, 'had brought with him, on leaving England, the section of a boat as a model to build from'. He described it as having been 'designed by a naval officer' of his acquaintance but it is clear from his untempered enthusiasm that it was his own idea of what a yacht should be. He had, of course, for two or three years, been a boy aboard ship as a midshipman, which is a kind of embryo 'naval officer'. No doubt it was in

Williams's mind that, once the thing had proved itself a magnificent success, there would come an entirely satisfactory moment when, with a blush, he would have to admit paternity. Of course, for most of his professional life he had been a cavalry officer, which does not sound like quite so good an endorsement for a ship-design, so perhaps he allowed the hazy notion to arise that somehow the design was just the sort of thing that was, or would have been, approved by the Admiralty. Or perhaps Mary just got hold of the wrong end of a stick that Williams did not even know he'd thrown. Words are unreliable things. That word 'model', for instance, as in 'section of a boat as a model to build from' and 'model taken from the Royal Dockyards' has led some writers to believe that what Williams had brought in his luggage was a kind of toy boat. Trelawny uses the word again, writing about the day that he had taken Shelley on a tour of the docks in Livorno. They were much taken with an American clipper.

'You must allow,' said Trelawny, 'that graceful craft was designed by a man who had a poet's feeling for things beautiful; let's get a model and build a boat like her.'

They went aboard and were cordially treated but, of course, they were no little replicas on sale and it had never crossed Trelawny's mind that there would be. This remark of Trelawny's – and the fact that he was, of course, a 'naval officer' – has led to yet more muddle in the grasping of sticks, so that you may find in print the idea that the supposed toy boat was not in Williams's luggage but Trelawny's and that Trelawny was the man behind the design of Shelley's fatal bark.

By 'model', of course, both Trelawny and Mary mean the

same thing: a detailed mental pattern or idea. Among people connected with making or building things according to a plan, architects, boat builders, engineers and many others, a 'section' is a detailed drawing in any one plane, as if the object in question had been sliced through. Common sections for boat – or, come to that, model – building will represent a lengthways slice through the construction from stem to stern. A plan will include as many transverse slices, at particular stations along the length, as the designer thinks necessary to represent the continuous change in shape from one end to the other. So Mary's 'model taken from the Royal Dockyards' means something Williams had down on paper and not something he lugged about made of wood.

So why, if he had harboured the plan so long in his mind and on paper, did it only now become a reality? That did have something to do with the arrival of Trelawny. Williams might have counted as pleasant and enthusiastic company. Trelawny was an altogether more formidable presence. Williams had a sort of boisterous energy. Trelawny was a force. Williams could make conversation. Trelawny was a spell-binder. Williams, too, was a family man, uxorious, with children. Trelawny was single, footloose and minded to adventure. Williams was a breeze and Trelawny was a wind that blew.

Mary tells us that 'Shelley's favourite taste was boating; when living near the Thames or by the Lake of Geneva, much of his life was spent on water. On the shore of every lake or stream or sea near which he dwelt, he had a boat moored.' All that was true and, lately, Williams had been his neighbour and companion and fellow sailor, pottering on the Serchio or, more adventurously, on the Arno. But, Mary goes on, almost in the same breath, 'Shelley's passion was the ocean; and he wished that our summers, instead of being passed among the hills near Pisa, should be spent on the shores of the sea.' If this was so, Shelley had been a long time turning his passion into action, which was hardly Shelley-like. True, the ocean had been in his poetry but the irresistible impulse, the 'passion' to bring it into his life came only after Trelawny arrived. Trelawny the spell-binder showed him real ships and told him sea-yarns. Trelawny gives the impression that it was he who let fly the idea of forming, with the Williamses, 'a colony on the Gulf of Spezia' where they would have 'all that reasonable people require'. They would have just the essentials – horses, books and boats – and would lead a simple life 'undisturbed by the botherations of the world'. It was, of course, a perfectly Shelleyan idea, absorbed at once. 'You can get Byron to come,' said Trelawny, but Shelley astutely improved on the suggestion. 'No,' he said, 'Byron is always influenced by his last acquaintance. You are the last man so do you pop the question.'

And so Trelawny, at least according to Trelawny, blew Byron into the scheme, too, and if Shelley was going to have a boat, Byron would have a bigger one. In fact, the idea of the little seaside colony had already been discussed before Trelawny arrived. The notion of having a boat built to complete the idyll was mentioned by Williams in the letter he wrote to seduce Trelawny down from Geneva and into the company at Pisa. All the same, once Trelawny arrived, the scheme began to roll with astonishing speed. Trelawny reached Pisa, and stepped into Shelley's life and Byron's, only on the 14th of January. The plans for the boats were discussed and passed back and forward before the final instructions were handed to Trelawny's friend, Captain Roberts, as agent in Genoa. The order to start building went to the shipyard on the 5th of February. The wind that suddenly came to scud them all along like that was Trelawny.

Beyond the broad specification, the actual lines and construction of Byron's vessel were left to the knowledge and discretion of Captain Roberts and the shipbuilders in Genoa. For Shelley's boat, they were expected to follow the lines of Williams's cherished plan. Both Captain Roberts and the shipwrights, as Trelawny remarks, 'protested against it'. She carried too much sail-area, not enough keel and a debatable amount of iron ballast. Even with two tons of it aboard, she was to prove, as they feared, *very crank in a breeze*. This is sailor talk for a boat far too ready to fall over sideways – to quote Admiral Smyth's always useful *Sailor's Word Book of 1867*: 'a vessel, by her construction or her stowage, inclined to lean over a great deal, or from insufficient ballast or cargo incapable of carrying sail without danger of overturning'.

Any kind of boat with sails up to catch the wind is naturally inclined to be blown over and common sense can easily see why. Translating common sense into simple physics, the mast is a lever and the wind in the sails is a force. To keep the boat somewhere near upright, some other force, using some other lever, will have to oppose them. A good weight somewhere below the waterline will do it. A ship of the line, as every visitor to HMS *Victory* learns, has a belly full of gravel. With yachts it is more often a weight in the form of an iron keel projecting below the hull. Whenever the wind acts to lever the boat over, it is also trying to lever the mass of keel or ballast upwards against the force of gravity. When a sailboat leans over so far, and no farther, in a given breeze, an agreement is being reached between the force of the wind and the force of gravity. The basis of the agreement should lie in the designer's calculations. If he decides not to have a deep keel, perhaps for the convenience of sailing in shallow waters, or so as to be able to draw the boat up on a beach, then to make up for lost leverage, more weight will be needed. How much more, and where, has to be calculated accordingly. As the head-shaking shipwrights suspected, the calculations in this case left something to be desired.

There was once a word in use for a boat or ship about which everything was, to the true sailor's mind, as also to his eye and hand, just plain right. 'Yare' was the word once used. It had its last real public outing in, I think, the film *High Society*, being bandied about improbably between Grace Kelly and, if I remember rightly, Bing Crosby in a floating love scene mawkishly crowned with the song 'True Love'.

The dictionary offers no negative of yare. Neither does it offer a special nautical word for a boat, like Shelley's, that is beautiful to the eye and quick but treacherously flawed. There ought to be such a word. It is amazing that there isn't. It would have been such a handy word for describing so many people. Or, for instance, cars. Shelley's *Don Juan*, after all, had much in common with James Dean's Porsche.

Let us dispose of the schooner-ketch-yawl question, being as sailor-like as we have to be and no more, because in disposing of the question we learn something about the fix that Shelley and Williams got themselves into and why they failed to get out of it alive. All these terms imply a sailing vessel with two masts. (Sometimes more, but let us not add rare and unnecessary complications.) The difference between a ketch and a yawl lies in whether the helmsman can see both masts or only one when he looks ahead. If it's only one and the other is behind his head, then he's aboard a yawl. If both masts are for'd of his nose, it's a ketch. The arrangement means that ketches are more likely to carry nearly equal amounts of sail on both masts, while yawls never do. In a yawl, the last carries less because too much sail too far back would create unbalanced pressures making a boat hard or impossible to handle, especially in a following wind. So *Don Juan*, with her more or less equal spread of sail on each mast, was not a yawl.

Nobody seems to care where the helmsman stations himself aboard a schooner. What matters to the nautical pedant is that the leading mast of a schooner is no taller than the mast standing aft and usually shorter. Like a ketch, a schooner may carry nearly equal amounts of sail on both masts, but if they are not equal, the first carries less.

Ignoring the fact that the schooners of New England also had a couple of square sails on yards to hoist as well, all the sails being discussed so far are of the kind called fore-and-aft. This is as self-explanatory as a sailor's term gets. It means that, whatever the shape of the sail, the whole length of one edge is attached to the mast and the rest goes towards the back of the boat. If you were to draw the profile of the whole vessel on a sheet of paper, you would happily be able to draw in the sail, nice and flat and pretty much its proper shape. You could also draw in the long timber, called a boom, to which the foot of the sail is attached. The leading end of the boom is connected to the mast by an arrangement that leaves it free to swing in an arc to either side of the vessel, so that the sailor can play with the angle the sails make to the wind. In this play lies all the mystery and mastery of sailing.

Back to the sheet of paper. The simplest sail that can be drawn is a single tall triangle, with its base along the boom and its apex at the top of the mast. Those who remember their school geometry will easily be able to calculate the area of this sail. Sail area, though, is power and, as men always want more of that, there is a trick to increase power by increasing the area. Consider that tall triangle again. Two of the sides are defined by those timber spars, the boom and the mast. A rope stretched from the top of the mast to the end of the boom would define the third side of the possible sail. To include more area, it is hard to adjust the spars, easy to fiddle with the rope. We could put up something like a clothes prop, with its foot attached somewhere up the mast, arrange it at a jaunty angle and use it to push that rope outwards. This would create quite a lot of extra area to be filled in with sail. The prop thing was invented by sailors long ago and is called a gaff. The extra area catches a bit more wind but at the cost of some complication. What used to be one sail now has to be two, a larger one below the gaff and a smaller one above, which sailors call a gaff-topsail. You get nothing for nothing in this world. The arrangement means more work to be done by the hands aboard. It also means more work to be done by gravity to balance the extra force of wind and so a bit more ballast is called for. This gaff rig, as it is called, also adds a lot of extra rope for getting everything up and down and generally making the sails do what is wanted. It also means more weight up aloft – extra sail, the wooden gaff, more tackle – to thrash about when things get difficult. With modern sailcloth and a better understanding of aerodynamics, the tall triangular sail, free of all that clutter, is much more efficient at squeezing power from the wind than gaffs and top'sls. The complications of the gaff rig are now the preserve of the romantic and the nostalgic who still find, when things get difficult, that there is plenty of work to be done, and it is all to be done in a hurry. Sailors of such yachts as these don't get caught with their pants down in a sudden blow. They get caught with their gaff top'sls up, urgently in need of getting them down.

All this goes for *Don Juan*. Indeed, it goes double, as she had two masts, gaff rigged. Ketch or schooner? Nautical pedantry rather misses the point. In Trelawny's usage the flavour of the word is more important than the conventions of rigging or anything else. A ketch sounds like something you might go out in to look at your lobster pots. A schooner is something else. Schooner was a word – is still a word – suggestive of a craft that skims the waves. It sounds as if there is a verb, somewhere, 'to schoon', that sounds as if it must mean something like skimming or bowling along. If there ever was such a verb nobody has tracked it down. 'Usually derived,' says the *Oxford Dictionary*, 'from a supposed New England verb *scoon* or *scun*.' The asterisks attached to those examples are the etymologist's polite cough meaning that he made them up. For Trelawny, as for Byron or Shelley, the word schooner (and what fool decided to stick the 'h' in?) had a particular flavour of its own to commend it. Its origin, as the *OED* tells us, is American. America – as they and all Americans saw it – was synonymous with Liberty.

After a quarter of a century of revolutionary wars, the dynasties of Europe were dancing on Bonaparte's grave, or they would have been had they not sent him to die in so God-forsaken and remote a corner as St Helena. Only in America had the reactionaries failed to douse the Promethean fire of Liberty. The American revolutionary war had been fought a decade and more before either poet's birth. That strange interlude in Anglo-American relations called the War of 1812, on the other hand, was a conflict that was still vivid in their minds. This was a war that used to be scrupulously omitted from our English school history books but was and is easy to find in American ones. It has nothing to do with the war that gave rise to Tchaikovsky's overture of the same name, involving the Grande Armée, the march on Moscow and so on. As wars go, it amounted to little more than a private spat between Britain and the United States. On land, it was a messy and inconclusive stalemate. At sea, though, the fledgling navy of the United States inflicted an altogether startling bloody nose on a Royal Navy that had grown used to thinking itself invincible. The New Englanders who built and manned USS *Constitution* had schooned about to great effect, not least on the day they engaged His Majesty's frigate *Java* and blew her out of the water, to their Lordships' great dismay. On the day that *Don Juan* arrived in the Gulf of Spezia, USS *Constitution*, 'Old Ironsides' herself, with her companion USS *Ontario*, was in the Mediterranean, showing the flag on her first cruise after a long refit. In June they would tie up at Livorno. Lord Byron would be delighted to find himself invited aboard as a guest of honour. Later, he would write of it with pleasure to Tom Moore.

> I have been invited on board of the American squadron, and treated with all possible honour and ceremony. They have asked me to sit for my picture; and, as I was going away, an American lady took a rose from me (which had been given to me by a very pretty Italian lady that very morning), because, she said, 'She was determined to send or take something which I had about me to America.' There is a kind of *Lalla Rookh* incident for you! However, all these American honours arise, perhaps, not so much from their enthusiasm for my 'Poeshie', as their belief in my dislike to the English – in which I have the satisfaction to coincide with them. I would rather, however, have a nod from an American, than a snuff-box from an emperor.

Things American and, especially, things that were both American and nautical were things that smacked of Liberty and recalled a poke in the eye for Liberty's great enemies, the rulers of Britain. What kind of radical would call a yacht a ketch when she could just as well be that much more admirable and American thing, a schooner? Of course she was a schooner.

* * *

Mr Heslop and his little delivery crew spoke 'most highly of her performances,' says Williams. It doesn't often happen that a delivery crew is allowed to hand over a brand-new yacht without reporting on how she sails. That report will not often be discouraging and this one wasn't. Still, the men added a note of caution that Williams does not bother to record. They mentioned it to Trelawny when they got back to Genoa.

> I despatched her under charge of two steady seamen, and a smart sailor lad . . . they told me on their return . . . that they had been out in a rough night, that she was a ticklish boat to manage, but had sailed and worked well, and with two good seamen she would do very well; and that they had cautioned the gents accordingly.

'With two good seamen . . . ' While Shelley was not a seaman and didn't fool himself that he was, he did believe that Williams was the real thing. The trouble was, so did Williams. He had some grounds for his self-belief. Although Williams had served nearly ten years in India as a cavalry officer in the service of the East India Company, on leaving Eton he had joined the Royal Navy as a midshipman, so his first uniform had been a naval one. He did not wear it long, but it was long enough for him to assume an air of comprehensive qualification in all things nautical. Trelawny was not altogether convinced:

> The boy was quick and handy, and used to boats. Williams was not as deficient as I anticipated, but over-anxious and wanted practice, which alone makes a man prompt in emergency. Shelley was intent on catching images from the ever-changing sea and sky, he heeded not the boat. On my suggesting the addition to their crew of a Genoese sailor accustomed to the coast – such as I had on board the *Bolivar* – Williams, thinking I under-valued his efficiency as a seaman, was scandalised – 'as if we three

seasoned salts were not enough to manage an open boat, when lubberly sloops and cutters of fifty or sixty tons were worked by as few men on the rough seas and iron-bound coast of Scotland!'

'Yes,' I answered, 'but what a difference between those sea-lions and you and our water-poet! A decked cutter besides, or even a frigate is easier handled in a gale or squall, and out-and-out safer to be on board of than an open boat. If we had been in a squall today, with the main-sheet jammed and the tiller put starboard instead of port, we should have had to swim for it.

Clearly there had been small adventures of incompetence. Still, Shelley had his own emergency procedure mapped out if it came to swimming.

'Not I! I should have gone down with the rest of the pigs in the bottom of the boat,' said Shelley, meaning the iron-pig ballast.

An inability to swim was possibly the only thing Shelley had in common with those 'sea-lions' of Scottish sailors. On that 'iron-bound' and gale-swept coast it has traditionally been thought a delusive skill that it were best not to acquire, as calculated only to prolong the last agonies of the unfortunate. Williams could swim. Within a month both men would, briefly, be in a position to make an informed but unrecordable comment on the wisdom of fishermen.

We should not read too much into what may seem an unconscious prophecy, as many have done, for all that there is something distinctively Shelleyan in it. Byron, famously, was a swimmer. Shelley, on the other hand, was known among his friends for his peculiar aptitude, when thrown into the water, for lying inert and sinking. He would lie on the bottom and imagine drowning until they dragged him up. So perhaps we should dismiss prophecy and just accept this as Shelley's boyish joke. Byron, after all, as Trelawny tells us, joked in much the same vein when they were all still in Pisa, dreaming adventures, while the boats were a-building in Genoa:

Shelley's boyish eagerness to possess the new toy, from which he anticipated never-failing pleasure in gliding over the azure seas, under the cloudless skies of an Italian summer, was pleasant to behold. His comrade Williams was inspired by the same spirit. We used to draw plans on the sands of the Arno of the exact dimensions of the boat, dividing her into compartments (the forepart was decked for stowage), and then, squatting down within the lines, I marked off the imaginary cabin.

With a real chart of the Mediterranean spread out before them, and with faces as grave and anxious as those of Columbus and his companions, they held councils as to the islands to be visited, coasts explored, courses steered, the amount of armament, stores, water and provisions which would be necessary. Then we would narrate instances of the daring of the old navigators, as when Diaz discovered the Cape of Good Hope in 1446, with two vessels each of fifty tons burthen; or when Drake went round the world, one of his craft being only thirty tons; and of the extraordinary runs and enterprises accomplished in open boats of equal or less tonnage than the one we were building, from the earliest times to those of Commodore Bligh. Byron, with the smile of a Mephistophiles standing by, asked me the amount of salvage we, the salvors, should be entitled to in the probable event of our picking up and towing Shelley's water-logged craft into port.

In the event, it was not Byron and Trelawny who would claim the salvage of *Don Juan* but Captain Roberts, the man now overseeing her building in the government yards in Genoa.

Certainly, the Genoese got on with the job. Perhaps, in the post-war depression, the order book was not so full or perhaps Roberts was just good at getting things done. Plans were still being passed back and forth in February but on the 12th of May, as we have seen, *Don Juan* rounded the headland of Porto Venere. Byron's much larger *Bolivar* would be delivered just a month later.

Monday, May 13th
Rain during night in torrents – a heavy gale of wind from S.W. and a surf running heavier than ever; at 4 gale unabated, violent squalls.

Not sailing weather, then, according to Williams, for the first day with their new plaything, but that wasn't going to keep them away from her.

Walked to Lerici with Shelley and went on board. Called on M. Maglian; and found him anxiously awaiting the moment of a third child's birth. In the evening an electric arch forming in the clouds announces a heavy thunder-storm, if the wind lulls. Distant thunder – gale increases – a circle of foam surrounds the bay – dark, rainy, and tempestuous, with flashes of lightning at intervals, which give us no hope of better weather. The learned in these things say that it generally lasts three days when once it commences as this has done. We all feel as if we were on board ship – and the roaring of the sea brings this idea to us even in our beds.

Tuesday, May 14th

Clear weather, and the breeze greatly moderated, contrary to all the expectations and the prophecies of these would-be sailors – these weather-wise landsmen. While dressing this morning, I saw the boat, under easy sail, bearing on and off land. At 9 we took her down, under top-sails and flying jib, to Spezzia; and, after tacking round some of the craft there, returned to Lerici in an hour and a half – a distance, they say, of four leagues. On our return, we were hailed by a servant of Count S—, a minister of the Emperor of Austria, who sent desiring to have a sail; but before he could get on board, the wind had lulled into a perfect calm, and we only got into the swell, and made him sick.

Wednesday, May 15th

Fine and fresh breeze in puffs from the land. Jane and Mary consent to take a sail. Run down to Porto Veneto [*sic*] and beat back at 1 o'clock. The boat sailed like a witch. After the late gale, the water is covered with purple nautili, or as the sailors call them, 'Portuguese men-of-war'. After dinner, Jane accompanied us to the point of the Magra; and the boat beat back in wonderful style.

It wasn't just Williams who was having a good time. Shelley thought *Don Juan* worth every penny and wrote to say as much to Trelawny.

Lerici, May 16, 1822

My Dear Trelawny,

The *Don Juan* is arrived, and nothing can exceed the admiration she has excited; for we must suppose the name to have been given her during the equivocation of sex which her godfather suffered in the harem. Williams declares her to be perfect, and I participate in his enthusiasm, inasmuch as would be decent in a landsman. We have been out now several days, although we have sought in vain for an opportunity of trying her against the feluccas or other large craft in the bay; she passes the small ones as a comet might pass the dullest planet of the heavens. When do you expect to be here in the *Bolivar*. If Roberts's £50 grow into a £500, and his ten days into months, I suppose I may expect that I am considerably in your debt, and that you will not be round here until the middle of the summer. I hope that I shall be mistaken in the last of these conclusions; as to the former, whatever may be the result, I have little reason and less inclination to complain of my bargain. I wish you could express from me to Roberts, how excessively I am obliged to him for the time and trouble he has expended for my advantage, and which I wish could be as easily repaid as the money which I owe him, and which I wait your orders for remitting.   S.

Shelley's Boat

Even Mary, far from pleased with Casa Magni, was pleased by little *Don Juan*. Not quite three weeks after her arrival – so Mary exaggerates a little in her letter – she wrote to Maria Gisborne, whose son, Henry, as it happened, was an aspiring marine engineer. She mentions the one glaring blemish that Shelley had tactfully not brought up in his letter to Trelawny.

Shelley's boat is a beautiful creature. Henry would admire her greatly – though only 24 feet by 8, she is a perfect little ship, and looks twice her size – She has one fault – she was to have been built in partnership with Williams and Trelawny – Trelawny chose the name of the *Don Juan* and we acceded; but when Shelley took her entirely on himself, we changed the name to the *Ariel* – Lord B chose to take fire at this, and determined she should be called after the poem – wrote to Roberts to have the name painted on the mainsail, and she arrived thus disfigured – for days and nights full twenty-one did Shelley and Edward ponder on her anabaptism, and the washing out of the primeval stain. Turpentine, spirits of wine, *buccata*, all were tried, and it became dappled and no more – at length the piece was taken out, and reefs put, so the sail does not look worse. I do not know what Lord B will say, but Lord and poet as he is, he could not be allowed to make a coal-barge of our boat.

Shelley, then, was delighted with *Don Juan* – in all but her name – and prepared to look cheerfully on the bill for the eighty pounds or so. Byron was to look at a bill ten times as big when *Bolivar* was delivered a month later. He did not put on a cheerful face about it. In fact, he was shocked, though it is hard to see why. He had not ordered a mere boat, after all.

Shelley's Boat

What he'd ordered was a little ship and that's what he got. He had even ordered her to be fitted with four brass cannon. If the bill upset Byron, it was the cannon that upset the authorities in Genoa, where they looked askance at the plans and reduced Byron's battery by two guns. But it wasn't the missing guns that took the gilt off the thing. Nor the bill, even if it did take a bit of swallowing. Had he still been in love with the idea, he might not have given the bill a second glance. The fact was that once the simple romantic idea had become a large and complicated reality, tied to the quay in Livorno and promising to make any number of mysterious and expensive demands on him, it exercised no seduction at all. The simple fact of her arrival compounded his already tiresome and exasperating relations with the Tuscan authorities. His politics were suspect and his mistress's family were classified as enemies of the state. Beyond that, there had been the little matter of an affray with the local soldiery in which he and others – Shelley included – had been involved. It should have been something and nothing – a sergeant-major of the local militia, Masi by name, had been ill-mannered in the street and needed rebuking. Some of Byron's servants had pitched in and been over-zealous in rebuking him with a dagger, or (as Byron reported the exaggerations, possibly exaggerating splendidly himself) possibly a pitchfork, or possibly a lance. Tita Falcieri was one of the suspected servants. It was this affair that had led to his expulsion from Pisa and his place on the household strength at Casa Magni. An inquiry was still in train. Charges were in the air. The *cancelliere* – the examining magistrate – had interviewed Byron and others in his circle several times. Now the turbulent English lord was taking delivery of a little ship with guns, a thing that pleased the Tuscan authorities no better than it had pleased the Genoese. An embargo was issued immediately. *Bolivar* was on no account to leave harbour without express and written permission from the port authorities.

Despite all this, Trelawny was delighted with the little ship now under his command and eager to introduce her to her owner and point out all her graces and advantages. But Byron had not been cradled in salt spray like his Cornish captain and, by this time, he had remembered as much. It is easy to imagine him, peering up her dizzying masts and letting his eye fuddle itself in the mysterious webs and skeins of her rigging. He was frank enough, as Trelawny remembers it.

'People think I must be a bit of a sailor from my writings. All the sea-terms I use are from authority, and they cost me time, toil and trouble to look them out; but you will find me a landlubber. I hardly know the stem from the stern, and don't know the name or use of a single rope or sail; I know the deep sea is blue, and not green, as that green-horn Shakespeare always calls it.'

Byron's remark about the deep blue sea prompts an irresistible digression to ask whether or not he was colour blind. There is an earlier conversation reported by Trelawny.

Byron looking at the western sky, exclaimed, 'Where is the green your friend the Laker talks such fustian about,' meaning Coleridge –

> Gazing on the western sky,
> And its peculiar tint of yellow green.

'Who ever,' asked Byron, 'saw a green sky?' Shelley was silent, knowing that if he replied, Byron would give vent to his spleen. So I said, 'The sky in England is oftener green than blue.'

'Black, you mean,' rejoined Byron; and this discussion brought us to his door.

A man who has never seen both red and green in a brilliant sunset is probably a man who can't tell them apart, the commonest form of colour-blindness, found mostly in men. If he was colour-blind he may not have cared to be told. When it came to sea-matters, Trelawny tells us, unequivocally, 'He neither knew nor cared to know, nor ever asked a question (except when writing) about sea-terms or sea-life.'

And in sea-matters, when looking at *Bolivar*, there is no mistaking Byron's tone. Here is a man who has sobered up. It is clear that there and then he decided to sell his costly new toy. Barely a fortnight after *Bolivar* arrived, Shelley tells us as much, in one of his last letters to Mary.

Pisa, July 4, 1822

My Dearest Mary,

I have received both your letters, and shall attend to the instructions they convey. I did not think of buying the *Bolivar*; Lord B. wishes to sell her, but I imagine would prefer ready money. I have as yet made no inquiries about houses near Pugnano . . .

When he wrote that, Shelley had just one short, final voyage left to make on *Don Juan*. As it happens, two days after his letter to Trelawny, in which he had been so cheerful about settling the bill, he had already come close to losing his investment. Or, rather, Williams, always the skipper, had nearly lost it for him. It is hard, reading Williams's journal, not to see an omen in the incident.

Saturday, May 18th
Fine fresh breeze. Sailed with Shelley to the outer island, and find that there is another small one beyond, which we have named the Sirens' rock. This name was chosen in consequence of hearing, at the time we were beating to windward to weather it, a sort of murmuring, which, as if by magic, seemed to proceed from all parts of our boat, now on the sea, now here, now there. At length we found that a very small rope (or cord rather) had been fastened to steady the peak when the boat was at anchor, and being drawn extremely tight with the weight of the sail, it vibrated as the wind freshened. Being on the other tack as we approached, it ceased, and again as we stood off it recommenced its song. The Sirens' island was well named; for standing in close to observe it, from a strong current setting towards it, the boat was actually attracted so close, that we had only time to tack, and save ourselves from its alluring voice.

'We had only time to tack, and save ourselves . . . ' The breathless tone is calculated to impress the hearer with a notion of his skill. He tells it as he might tell of an adventure on the hunting field, of how he'd suddenly had to spur his horse to clear some unexpected ditch at full gallop. A sailor more honest with himself, or perhaps just more intelligent than Williams, would have realised that the quirky humming of a rope was not the most interesting thing about the excursion. What called for notice was that his poor seamanship had come within an ace of putting them on the rocks. But that kind of reflection would have admitted some boundary to his boundless self-confidence and was, therefore, not easy for him. Williams could not learn from other people because he genuinely believed he always knew better. He could not learn from his own mistakes because he could not recognise them. In the man in whom Shelley placed his entire trust when afloat, it was to be – as on the 16th of May it had come close to being – a fatal flaw. His virtue remained his enthusiasm, his eagerness to be up and doing; his vice, ignorance of himself.

Wednesday, May 22d
Fine, after a threatening night. After breakfast Shelley and I amused ourselves with trying to make a boat of canvas and reeds, as light and as small as possible – she is to be eight and a half feet long, and four and a half broad.

It wasn't the first time they'd built one of these little craft, something between a dinghy and a coracle. They'd made one the summer before, as Mary remembered in her notes, editing the poems of 1821.

There are no pleasure-boats on the Arno; and the shallowness of its waters (except in wintertime, when the stream is too turbid and impetuous for boating) rendered it difficult to get any skiff light enough to float. Shelley, however, overcame the difficulty; he, together with a friend, contrived a boat such as the huntsmen carry about with them in the Maremma, to cross the sluggish but deep streams that intersect the forests – a boat of laths and pitched canvas. It held three persons and he was often seen on the Arno in it, to the horror of the Italians, who remonstrated on the danger, and could not understand how anyone could take pleasure in an exercise that risked life. 'Ma va per la vita!' they exclaimed.

Sunday, May 26th

Cloudy. Rose at six, and went with Shelley and Maglian to Massa. The landing-place, or rather the beach, which is about three miles from the town, affords no kind of shelter, but where there is a continued sea running. A little to the left of the second gun-battery, is a shelf running parallel to the beach, at the termination of which five feet of water may be had. This shelf is indicated by the shortness and frequency of the surf, and the deep water by a partial cessation of it. It is necessary before any effort is made to work her in – to send a strong sternfast on shore for this purpose, as the current of the Magra sets forcibly to the eastward, and sweeps her suddenly into the surf beyond. We dined at Massa, and left it again at ten minutes past four, with a strong westerly wind straight in our teeth. This wind (the *Ponente* as it is called) always sends a damp vapour from the sea, which gathers into watery clouds on the mountain tops, and generally sinks with the sun, but strengthens as he declines. To the landing-place it is said to be fifteen miles to Lerici. We left the latter place at a little past eight and arrived at eleven, and returned in seven hours.

Shelley's Boat

Thursday, June 6th

Calm. Left Villa Magni, at five, on our way to Via Reggio. At eight the wind sprung up, baffling in all directions but the right one. At eleven we could steer our course; but at one it fell calm, and left us like a log on the water, but four miles to windward of Massa. We remained there till six; the thunder-clouds gathering on the mountains around, and threatening to burst in squalls; heat excessive. At seven rowed into Massa beach – but on attempting to land we were opposed by the guard, who told us that the head person of the fort (of two rusty guns) being at Festa, that, as he was not able to read, we must wait till the former arrived. Not willing to put up with such treatment, Shelley told him at his peril to detain us, when the fellow brought down two old muskets, and we prepared our pistols, which he no sooner saw we were determined to use, than he called our servant to the beach, and desiring him to hold the paper about a yard from him, he suffered two gentlemen who were bathing near the place to explain who and what we were. Upon this, the fellow's tone changed from presumption to the most cowardly fawning, and we proceeded to Massa unmolested. Slept at Massa, about three miles inland.

The scene is at least as absurd and delightful as anything in a comic-opera but no one should think that there was something automatically laughable about Shelley with a gun. He was, as it happens, an excellent shot. He used to practise. In his walks near Marlow with Hunt or Peacock, he always took his pistols for pot-shots along the way and

Pisan afternoons were often wiled away in contests with Byron, Trelawny and the rest.

The fact that the beach was guarded at all tells us something about the times. We have seen the state of the country the Shelleys left behind. The country they had come to was no less turbulent and far more disorganised. Italy as a nation had, indeed, yet to be organised at all. In 1822, it was a mere geographical expression. The idea that it might become something more than that had begun to burn in certain hearts and minds but those minds had played no part in the Congress of Vienna, in 1815, when the powers that had defeated Napoleon sat down to remake Europe. Italy had been carved up and served round like a buffet lunch. Naples and Sicily were once again united under Bourbon rule. Parma, Piacenza and Guastalla were handed to the French, to be the personal duchies of the Empress Marie Louise. The Pope was restored to the throne of his earthly territories and the house of Hapsburg-Lorraine got back Tuscany and Modena. The hosts lost the Netherlands but, by way of compensation, were given Lombardy and the Veneto. The kingdom of Sardinia was restored, to rule over Savoy, Piedmont and the Ligurian littoral, including Nice and Genoa.

The repressive laws and harsh taxes of the new or re-invented regimes coincided with Nature's conspiracy of climatic crisis, crop failures and famine. In Italy's world of subsistence agriculture, the effects were even more disastrous than in England's world of surpluses, specialisations and modern industries. From buffet lunch, Italy had degenerated to dog's breakfast. A resistance to the rule of foreign powers and tin-pot courts grew, fostered by the secret society of the Carbonari – a kind of international freemasonry of republicans – and attracting young men like Mazzini, proclaiming their loyalty to a state that did not yet exist, a unified Italy. The Risorgimento had begun. (Quite what was resurgent is hard to say, as Italy had never before been a unified state. The nearest thing might have been the Roman Empire but that, after all, was Roman, not Italian.)

In 1820, there had been a military coup to be placated in Naples, a workers' revolt to be crushed in Palermo, another in Piedmont the following year. Trelawny said that Lord Byron 'never drew his weapon to redress any wrongs but his own', but if he did not draw either sword or pen in Italy's cause, he was true enough to his angry radical ideals to become involved, if only through the intrigues of his mistress's family. He put up money for guns and, it seems, allowed weapons to be cached in his palazzo. It did not go unnoticed. A cardinal recorded his suspicions, concerning the Naples coup, that the 'well-known Lord Byron' was 'suspected of complicity in this bold plot'.

Friday, June 7th
Left Massa at half-past five – a dead calm, the atmosphere hot and oppressive. At eight a breeze sprung up, which enabled us to lie up to Magra Point. Beat round the point and reached home at half-past two.

It had taken up odd scraps of time over three weeks or so, but the little tender that they had been building 'out of canvas and reeds', had finally taken shape and was finished. It was going to make them more independent. They would be able to row themselves ashore from shallow anchorages. It would extend the range and freedom of their adventures. Williams, of course, was pleased with what must have been mostly his own work.

Wednesday, June 12th
Launched the little boat, which answered our wishes and expectations. She is 86 lbs English weight, and stows easily on board.

A month later, the fishermen at Viareggio would tell Trelawny of a little punt washed up, together with a barrel and some bottles. He would see it, this little tender, the handiwork of Williams and a little of Shelley's, too, and he would know it at once. It would tell him all that he did not want to know. In the middle of June, though, the little boat was new-born into an idyll. It may be that by the end of the day Jane might have wished that her husband had been less eager for her to admire and enjoy the new toy.

Sailed in the evening, but were becalmed in the offing, and left there with a long ground swell, which made Jane little better than dead. Hoisted out our little boat and brought her on shore. Her landing attended by the whole village.

Thursday, June 13th
Fine. At nine, saw a vessel between the straits of Porto Venere like a man-of-war brig. She proved to be the *Bolivar*, with Roberts and Trelawny on board, who are taking her round to Livorno. On meeting them we were saluted by six guns. Sailed together to try the vessels – in

speed no chance with her, but I think we keep as good a wind. She is the most beautiful craft I ever saw, and will do more for her size. She costs Lord Byron £750 clear off and ready for sea, with provisions and conveniences of every kind.

Trelawny, in his recollections seems to misremember the sequence of dates, but this must have been the day that he made an outing across the bay with Shelley and Williams and the same day that he and Shelley had a strange conversation about death. Trelawny's style is always colourful and his stories are always told tall (Buffon is right on the money with Trelawny), but there can be no doubt that the vivid picture in his *Recollections* tells us how it was aboard *Don Juan*.

Not long after, I followed in Byron's boat, the *Bolivar* schooner. There was no fault to find with her, Roberts and the builder had fashioned her after their own fancy, and she was both fast and safe. I manned her with five able seamen, four Genoese and one Englishman. I put into the Gulf of Spezzia, and found Shelley in ecstasy with his boat, and Williams as touchy about her reputation as if she had been his wife. They were hardly ever out of her, and talked of the Mediterranean as a lake too confined and tranquil to exhibit her sea-going excellence. They longed to be on the broad Atlantic, scudding under bare poles in a heavy sou'wester, with plenty of sea room. I went out for a sail in Shelley's boat to see how they would manage her. It was great fun to witness Williams teaching the Poet how to steer, and other points of seamanship. As usual, Shelley had a book in hand, saying he could read and steer at the same time, as one was mental, the other mechanical.

'Luff!' said Williams.

'Luff'. The term is in use, unchanged, to this day. Admiral Smyth defines it: 'the order to the helmsman to bring the ship's head up more to windward'. That's not what Shelley did.

Shelley put the helm the wrong way. Williams corrected him.

'Do you see those two white objects ahead? keep them in a line, the wind is heading us.' Then, turning to me, he said: 'Lend me a hand to haul in the main-sheet, and I will show you how close she can lay to the wind to work off a lee-shore.'

'No,' I answered, 'I am a passenger, and won't touch a rope.'

'Luff!' said Williams, as the boat was yawing about. 'Shelley, you can't steer, you have got her in the wind's eye; give me the tiller, and you attend the main-sheet. Ready about!' said Williams. 'Helms down – let go the fore-sheet – see how she spins round on her heel – is not she a beauty? Now, Shelley, let go the main-sheet and, boy, haul aft the jib-sheet!'

The main-sheet was jammed, and the boat unmanageable, or as sailors express it, in irons; when the two had cleared it, Shelley's hat was knocked overboard, and he would probably have followed, if I had not held him. He was so uncommonly awkward, that when they had things shipshape, Williams, somewhat scandalised at the lubberly manoeuvre, blew up the Poet for his neglect and inattention to orders. Shelley was, however, so happy and in such high glee, and the nautical terms so tickled his fancy, that he even put his beloved Plato in his pocket, and gave his mind up to fun and frolic.

'You will do no good with Shelley,' I said, 'until you heave his books and papers overboard; shear the wisps of hair that hang over his eyes; and plunge his arms up to the elbows in a tar-bucket. And you, captain, will have no authority, until you dowse your frock-coat and cavalry boots. You see I am stripped for a swim, so please, whilst I am on board, to keep within swimming distance of the land.'

After this outing there were days when there was to be no sailing and no more than ten or a dozen days on which Shelley might have become less cack-handed or Williams come to be as handy as 'the boy' Vivian. You have to wonder how much things could possibly have improved in so short a time. Still, anything to do with the little boat seemed to make Shelley cheerful. He was even cheerful about meeting the bills in the letter that he sent chasing after Trelawny, as he and *Bolivar* continued their trip to Livorno, At least, he begins cheerfully.

18th June

I have written to Guelhard, to pay you 154 Tuscan crowns, the amount of the balance against me according to Roberts's calculation, which I keep for your satis-faction, deducting sixty, which I paid the *aubergiste* at Pisa, in all 214. We saw you about eight miles in the offing this morning; but the abatement of the breeze leaves us little hope that you can have made Leghorn this evening. Pray write us a full, true, and particular account of your proceedings, &c. – How Lord Byron likes the vessel; what are your arrangements and intentions for the summer; and when we may expect to see you or him in this region again; and especially whether there is any news of Hunt.

Roberts and Williams are very busy in refitting the *Don Juan*; they seem determined that she shall enter Leghorn in style. I am no great judge of these matters; but am excessively obliged to the former, and delighted that the latter should find amusement, like the sparrow, in educating the cuckoo's young.

The tone of brisk business and breezy chat cannot have prepared Trelawny for what was a sudden shift in mood and matter, even by Shelley's mercurial standards.

You, of course, enter into society at Leghorn: should you meet with any scientific person, capable of preparing the Prussic Acid, or essential oil of bitter almonds, I should regard it as a great kindness if you could procure me a small quantity.

It requires the greatest caution in preparation, and ought to be highly concentrated; I would give any price for this medicine; you remember we talked of it the other night, and we both expressed a wish to possess it; my wish was serious, and sprung from the desire of avoiding needless suffering. I need not tell you I have no intention of suicide at present, but I confess it would be a comfort to me to hold in my possession that golden key to the chamber of perpetual rest. The Prussic Acid is used in medicine in Infinitely minute doses; but that preparation is weak, and has not the concentration necessary to medicine all ills infallibly. A single drop, even less, is a dose, and it acts by paralysis.

I am curious to hear of this publication about Lord Byron and the Pisa circle. I hope it will not annoy him, as to me I am supremely indifferent. If you have not shown the letter I sent you, don't, until Hunt's arrival, when we shall certainly meet.

Your very sincere friend,

P. B. SHELLEY

Mary is better, though still excessively weak.

Mary, the mere postscript, was weak because she had come close to death. Two days before, she had miscarried. She had bled and bled. Casa Magni today is larger than it was then. The rear has been extended and, according to the brass plates beside the door of that extension, you might nowadays have a choice of medical practitioners. The cardiologist might be a good pick. In 1822 the nearest doctor was rather further away. Probably in La Spezia. She bled and bled and began to slip into that state of weak heedlessness where the slope to death begins to steepen unmistakably. For seven hours they kept her from losing consciousness by ringing changes with vinegar, brandy, eau-de-Cologne.

Shelley did the doctoring, adapting the principle you might use to stop a nosebleed but adjusting the scale of things to match the scale of the bleeding. He sent for ice. Given that the nearest loaf of bread was three kilometres away, it might seem odd that so sophisticated a commodity as ice was to be had, somewhere close enough to hand, in the middle of a June heatwave in this primitive landscape. There were no landed gentry with ice houses in the deep-delved earth on this coast. A guess, then, is that in Lerici they stored winter ice from the hills, not for cooling wine or making sorbets, but to keep their fish marketable, and that it was the local fish-buyer who supplied the ice. With no doctor to advise them, Claire and Jane were afraid of using it. Shelley, in Mary's words, 'overruled them & by an unsparing application of it, I was restored'. It worked. Mary was to live another thirty years. Shelley was to live another twenty-three days.

While Shelley was busy saving Mary from death and, momentarily at least, contemplating his own, Williams, as Shelley had mentioned, found himself something to do. Something practical. Out of the house.

Wednesday, June 19th
Fine . . . Took the ballast out and hauled the boat on the beach. Cleaned and greased her.

Thursday, June 20th
Fine. Shelley hears from Hunt that he is arrived at Genoa having sailed from England on the 13th May.

Saturday, June 22d
Calm. Heat overpowering, but in the shade refreshed by the sea breeze. At seven launched our boat, with all her ballast in. She floats three inches lighter than before. This difference is caused, I imagine, by her planks having dried while on shore.

Shelley's Boat

Williams is wonderfully complacent. In the previous few days he has been busy. With help from Roberts, he has changed the rigging of *Don Juan*, adding a little height to the masts to increase the sail she might carry. No doubt, after the shakedown trials around the bay, there was also a good deal of lesser tinkering. It's the sort of thing those who sail for pleasure love to do, changing the arrangement of all those things the rest of us just call ropes: halyards, sheets, down-hauls, stays, preventers and God knows what, always looking for a little more effect for a little less cause, and quite often getting the equation arse about. According to some reports, they made her a little longer by adding a false stern, a trick that may increase, at least in theory, a boat's maximum speed. The most satisfying modification may have been cutting out that high-handed caprice of Byron's from the mainsail. A blank and blameless patch was stitched in. She was *Don Juan* no longer. After all this, they relaunched her. She rode three inches higher out of the water than before. As they had added a certain amount of weight, all other things being equal, she should have sat a fraction lower. She rode higher. Three inches may sound negligible, and it clearly wasn't enough to worry Williams overmuch. It should have been. In a boat already known to be 'crank', it should have cost him a little sleep.

Ariel, as we may now properly call her – and will from now on – was displacing less water than before by three inches. As a floating body displaces exactly its own weight in water, we can make a rough calculation from that three inches how much weight the boat had lost. If we could slice the boat apart right along the waterline, we would see the size and shape of her footprint on the water. A reasonable guess at the size of that footprint, in the case of a twenty-four-foot-long gentleman's yacht, eight feet in the beam, might be one hundred square feet. As three inches is a quarter of a foot, it's not hard to arrive at a change in displacement of twenty-five cubic feet. This is how much less water *Ariel* was pushing out of the way than she had been pushing out of the way under the name of *Don Juan*. Water weighs fifty-six pounds per cubic foot. Archimedes would have told Williams that somewhere or other, during the last few days, his boat had lost about fourteen hundred pounds. Nearly three quarters of a ton. Perhaps our calculations are too generous. Perhaps the change wasn't quite three inches. Perhaps the footprint is only eighty square feet or less. So perhaps the loss was only half a ton.

Only?

Williams imagined it was water lost from the planks because the weather was hot and perhaps the timbers had lost some moisture. But half a ton of it? Maybe there was somewhere else to look for the lost weight.

Her builders had found that she needed two and a half tons of ballast in her bottom, in the form of those pigs of cast-iron that Shelley made his joke about going to the bottom with. Before they had her hauled up the beach at Lerici, the pigs came out and must have been stacked somewhere handy. Roberts and Williams, officers and gentlemen both, will not have shifted lumps of iron when, for a few quattrini, a bunch of local hands could be detached from sewing nets and set to that kind of thing. They must have recruited hands, anyway, to help in unstepping the masts and generally heaving her out of the water. The same hands would have helped to restep the masts and, of course, ship the ballast again. A lump of iron is a valuable thing. In a little, poverty-stricken, maritime community accustomed to use rocks for ballast, a lump of iron is a thing both useful and attractive. Seductive, almost. Seeing her floating three inches lighter, Williams, always confident, thought he knew the answer. He imagined water had evaporated from the planks. Archimedes would have counted the pigs. But Archimedes was not at Lerici when she went back into the water and it seems a fair bet that Captain Roberts wasn't either. It is not likely that he could have shrugged those three inches away quite so easily. She had been, as the delivery crew told Trelawny, 'a ticklish boat to handle'. Well, now she was going to be even more ticklish.

Eight

Thursday, June 27th

Fine. The heat increases daily, and prayers are offering for rain. At Parma, it is now so excessive that the labourers are forbidden to work in the fields after ten and before five, fearful of an epidemic.

For the first time, we find a note of wider awareness in Williams's diary. It is fitting enough. In a matter of days, that pervasive fear, that dread of epidemic, would have its say in the disposal of his own last remains.

From Trelawny we learn how well Lord Byron's way of life was adapted to such a climate.

> So far as I could learn from Fletcher, his yeoman bold – and he had been with him from the time of his first leaving England – Byron wherever he was, so far as it was practicable, pursued the same lazy, dawdling habits he continued during the time I knew him. He was seldom out of his bed before noon, when he drank a cup of very strong green tea, without sugar or milk. At two he ate a biscuit and drank soda-water. At three he mounted his horse and sauntered along the road – and generally the same road – if alone, racking his brains for fitting matter and rhymes for the coming poem, he dined at seven, as frugally as anchorites are said in story-books to have done, at nine he visited the family of Count Gamba, on his

return home he sat reading or composing until two or three o'clock in the morning, and then to bed, often feverish, restless and exhausted – to dream, as he said, more than to sleep.

If there is more than a little of the adolescent in Byron's routine, we should not be too surprised. Though he went no more a-roving, Byron still thought of himself as the stuff of which Regency bucks were made, and, in exile, he may have been one of the last examples of the genuine article. It was the expatriate's fate, in Trelawny's opinion. Byron had been out of England too long to know how the fashion had moved on. Still, Byron would not be the last man in the world to believe the first article of the buck's creed: that perpetual adolescence is the greatest privilege that money can buy and rank excuse. The frugal meals were not a sign of a new, ascetic, maturity. The fact was, as he approached his mid-thirties, that he had begun to run to fat and the fact dismayed him. He knew it was most un-Byronic. As Hunt hove up, he was sitting for his portrait by the American artist William West, and he had sat for his bust by Bartolini earlier in the year. He knew how he ought to be painted or sculpted. And it wasn't fat.

A man who has little business other than attending to his own pleasure is apt to find the intrusion of other people's business vexatious. Largely thanks to Shelley, other people's business was about to intrude on Byron with a vengeance. It was not just Leigh Hunt who was in the offing. It was Hunt, his wife Marianne and their six unruly children.

Word that the Hunts had at last reached Genoa had come while Williams was engrossed in the refit of *Ariel*. It was news

Shelley had been waiting and asking for. Hunt, always his staunchest friend in England, was what we might nowadays call a campaigning editor. With his brother John as partner, he had published, written for and edited the *Examiner*, an unabashed radical review in which they offended against political decency by drawing attention to such things as the brutality of military floggings or, even more indecently, to the wretched poverty which was the reward of the cannon-fodder class once they were no longer required to bleed and die and be heroes. The *Examiner* had also outraged the Prince Regent by publishing many wicked things about him, all true, and by calling him, among other things, 'a fat Adonis' of fifty. In its heyday, the better part of a decade earlier, the *Examiner* had landed the Hunt brothers in jail for two years. Short of dying for his principles, a radical can hardly do more than suffer imprisonment for them, and Shelley loved him for it. Even Byron had been to visit him in jail. It was their only previous meeting.

The prospect of seeing Hunt again gladdened Shelley's heart but it was also a matter of great anxiety to him. Inviting Hunt to come to Italy had been Shelley's idea but Byron had been all for it – at the time. He had been toying with the idea of starting a radical review on his own account and had thought of calling it *I Carbonari*. In 1820, you couldn't really have come up with a more explicit title. Today's equivalent might be *FLN Guerrilla*. That idea, not surprisingly, had been stillborn but from that starting point Shelley had talked him into the proposed collaboration with Hunt, the experienced editor, and generally egged on both men. He saw himself as 'a sort of link' to bring the 'two thunderbolts together'.

Shelley's Boat

Byron had even joined with Shelley in putting up the money to enable the impoverished Hunt to make the journey. The idea was that both of them should lend their names and their pens to Hunt's projected new journal. The important pen, of course, would be Byron's. He was the big name, the bestseller. With Byron on board, the journal would have every hope of success. Though Shelley would write for the magazine, the profits, if any, were to be divided between Hunt and Byron. The 'if any' was a wise caveat. Shelley wrote to Hunt telling him to make sure he had some other means of support before leaving England for Italy, and not to rely entirely on the future and doubtful profits of the magazine that was now to be called the *Liberal*. Hunt had not been wise enough to take Shelley's advice. Worse still, he had given up his connection with the *Examiner*.

For Hunt, then, this new venture was something close to a desperate hope. It was almost a year since it had been conceived, yet so far it did not amount even to an embryo. It was Shelley's fear that his friend had come so far only to find his journal, and his hopes, aborted by Byron. Influenced by some self-interested dissuasion from his publisher, Byron's commitment was on the wane and Shelley knew it.

One of the reasons Shelley had been so anxious to hear word of Hunt's arrival was that he knew that Byron was on the point of leaving Pisa and nobody, not even Byron, knew where he would be leaving for. Byron being Byron, it was always possible that he would suddenly disappear, like one of his own characters, in the swirl of a cape and a clatter of hooves. Trelawny had been told to investigate the possibility of transporting *Bolivar* overland to Lake Geneva but there was also talk of going to North America. Or South America. And many another place.

Hunt and his family had set out from England as long ago as the previous November, but November is a bad month to be heading west down the English Channel. Their ship had been beaten about by storms and got no farther than Dartmouth. The voyage had been abandoned. They had retreated to winter quarters in Plymouth, eating up the money that Shelley had sent. For one reason or another they did not start out again until the 13th of May, the day after *Ariel*, under the alias of *Don Juan*, had been delivered to Lerici. Eight months after beginning their journey, exhausted and broke, with six children and a desperately ill wife on his hands, Hunt must have drawn towards Pisa with the feelings of a desert wanderer who has at last glimpsed the palm tops of an oasis. Mary had written a most beckoning picture of the apartment on the *piano terreno* of the Lanfranchi palazzo that Byron had made over for their use. Mary and Shelley together had furnished and made it ready for them. If it weren't for Marianne's being so ill, he might reasonably have thought that all his trials would soon be over.

He had no idea how bad his timing was.

It wasn't just a question of Byron's mercurial temperament. It was that Masi business back in March. He hadn't died of pitchfork wounds, or whatever they were, after all, but the Tuscan authorities were not going to let the matter drop. Of course they wouldn't, because politics was involved. Masi had been responsible for the whole thing, deliberately galloping his horse through the sedate party of mounted Englishmen – Byron and his entourage with their ladies behind them in a carriage – returning from their habitual afternoon ride outside the city. Masi's behaviour was taken for damned insolence, which was just what he meant it to be. To their protests he returned insults. Some of the party had caught up with him, at which he had drawn his sabre and started to lay about him, injuring Captain Hay badly enough and very nearly doing the same to Shelley. At the city gates he'd called out his men to arrest the Englishmen but with variable success. Byron had simply ridden through the guard but others – Captain Hay for one – were seized, so Byron had returned, white with fury. The trouble was that the uniform of a sergeant-major in the Tuscan militia was such a fine and dandy affair that Byron had made the mistake of taking Masi for an officer. Though armed, at the time, with nothing more than his cane, he had offered the Italian 'his hand and glove thereon'. Masi had declined to pick up the gauntlet. He had ridden off. Then a couple of Byron's over-enthusiastic servants had waylaid him with that pitchfork. And so on.

And on and on. It had all happened back in March. When Hunt arrived on the last day of June the dust had not settled and the consequences had magnified.

Mary had written out the fair copy of Byron's statement. (Her more usual task, at the time, was making fair copies of the cantos of *Don Juan*.) But the police kept coming to the Lanfranchi Palace. There had been a court appearance. Four of Byron's servants had been arrested, and two, including Tita Falcieri, had been held in solitary confinement. A crowd of Pisans, with suspicious theatricality, had filled the street demanding their blood or their exile or a combination of the two. The rented mob is not a recent invention. All of this was tedious in itself but it was the cue for worse. The Tuscan government put it, or chose to put it, all down to radical troublemaking by the house of Gamba and decided it was time to ask them to leave. With his mistress and her father forced to move out of Pisa and find somewhere else to live, both love and honour obliged Byron to join them in their exodus.

Pisa, July 4th 1822

To E. J. DAWKINS [British Minister at Florence]

Dear Sir – I regret to say that my anticipations were well founded. The Gamba family received on Tuesday an order to quit the Tuscan States in four days. Of course this is virtually my own exile, for where they go I am no less bound by honour than by feeling to follow. I believe we shall try to obtain leave to remain at Lucca – if that fails, Genoa – and, failing that, possibly America; for both Captain Chauncey of the American Squadron (which returns in September) and Mr Bruen an American Merchant man at Leghorn offered me a passage in the handsomest manner – the latter sent to me to say that he would even send his vessel round to Genoa for us, if we chose to accept his offer. With regard to the interpretation which will be put upon my departure at this time, I hope that you will do me the favour of letting the truth be known, as my own absence will deprive me of the power of doing so for myself, and I have little doubt that advantage will be taken of that circumstance.

This letter will be presented to you by Mr Taaffe, who is in considerable confusion at a measure to which his own heedlessness has a good deal contributed. But – poor fellow – I suppose that he meant no harm. He wanted the Countess Guiccioli to go to Florence and fling herself at the feet of the Grand Duchess –

> a supplicant to wait
> While Ladies interpose, and Slaves debate.

I can only say, that if she did anything of the kind, I would never fling myself at her feet again.

Collini's office has now become a Sinecure, and I wish him joy of it. The inconvenience and expense to me will be very considerable, as I have two houses, furniture, Wines, Dinner Services – linen, – books, my Schooner – and in short – a whole establishment for a family – to leave at a moment's warning and this without knowing where the Gambas will be permitted to rest, and of course where I can rest also.

The whole thing – the manner in which it was announced, by the Commissary etc. was done in the most insulting manner. The Courier treated as if he were a delinquent, and sent away with Soldiers to take charge of him and lodged in the prison of Pisa, by way of Hostel.

I trust that this just Government is now content, my countrymen have been insulted and wounded by a rascal, and my Servants treated like Criminals though guiltless while a noble and respectable family including a sick lady are ordered away like so many felons, without a shadow of justice, or even a pretence of proof.

He might have added, ' . . . and Leigh Hunt has just turned up with no money, a wife they say is dying and a project concerning a magazine in which I am supposed to take an interest. Oh, and six undisciplined brats whom I am learning to loathe.'

No. It was not good timing and Shelley knew it. He had worked to bring what he called 'the two thunderbolts' together. He now had to be there to manage the potentially explosive meeting. For the first time in her brief career, *Ariel* ceased to be a toy and became a means of transport. As long as the wind blew in their favour, she provided the quickest way to reach Livorno. Judging by Mary's recollection of their speed, the winds held good.

> On the 1st of July they left us. If ever shadow of future ill darkened the present hour, such was over my mind when they went. During the whole of our stay in Lerici, an intense presentiment of coming evil brooded over my mind, and covered this beautiful place and genial summer with the shadow of coming misery. I had vainly struggled with these emotions – they seemed accounted for by my illness; but at this hour of separation they recurred with renewed violence. I did not anticipate danger for them, but a vague expectation of evil shook me to agony, and I could scarcely bring myself to let them go. The day was fine and clear; and, a fine breeze rising at twelve, they weighed for Leghorn. They made the run of about fifty miles in seven hours and a half. The *Bolivar* was in port; and, the regulations of the Health-office not permitting them to go on shore after sunset, they borrowed cushions from the larger vessel, and slept on board their boat.

The following morning, Shelley took the Hunts from

Livorno to Pisa to usher them into the Lanfranchi palazzo. For the second time in a month he found himself with a desperately sick woman on his hands, but at least in Pisa there was the excellent Dr Vacca to call in. The Shelleys had faith in Vacca – it was his fame, after all, that had made them feel comfortable choosing Pisa as a place to live – but his prognosis was as discouraging as it could very well be. Marianne's case was hopeless, he believed. She was going to die and they should be resigned to the fact. He prescribed a course of treatment, all the same, just in case there should be any slight chance that he might be wrong. As it would turn out, Marianne Hunt would survive and live to ripe old age. It's hard to know whether to criticise Vacca for the pessimistic prognosis or give him credit for the treatment in which he had so little faith. We might as well leave him with his reputation. The doctor with only limited belief in his medicines is at least to be preferred to the pedlar of miracle cures.

Marianne's condition and Vacca's opinion threw a pall of gloom and anxiety over a meeting in which so much hope had been invested. It didn't help that Byron seemed to be graceless and unwelcoming to Hunt's wife. 'He scarcely deigned to notice her; was silent, and scarcely bowed,' is how Williams reported it, second-hand from Shelley. Hunt, always quick to take offence if he thought he was being looked down on, was cut to the quick. He put Byron's attitude down to the coldness of his lordship's high and mighty snobbery. But then, it was so obviously true that Byron was a snob that one wonders how Hunt could have arrived at Pisa under any other impression.

It is, though, worth taking an alternative view of that

somewhat distant nod from Byron to Marianne Hunt. In this heatwave, labourers had been forbidden to work in the fields in the worst of the day's heat 'for fear of an epidemic'. However doubtful the science, the fear of epidemic was real and reasonable. Perhaps Hunt did not know that he and Marianne were lucky not to have been quarantined for forty days. Perhaps he did not know that Byron's daughter had just died of typhus. He surely did not consider for a moment how Byron might have viewed the complication of having a more or less destitute family of eight and a disease – whatever it was – suddenly take up quite so much of a house that he was, more or less, under orders to quit.

Nine

As in many a drama drawing towards its inevitable crisis, the cast is now divided into two groups in different locations. Three women, Mary, Claire and Jane, were left at San Terenzo. The eldest was not yet twenty-five years of age but they had more in common than youth. Though only two had children living, all were mothers. Only one had an extraordinary gift but none was without her measure of talent. Only one would have been thought truly remarkable for her looks but none was without her measure of beauty. Beyond these things, they had something in common that was rare and strange. After all, an Englishwoman who had arrived at the lunatic's folly, Casa Magni, that remote, seductive yet alarming shell of a house, half ruined on a rocky shore, and had made her bed above its sandy, sea-washed floor, was an Englishwoman who had followed an unusual and daring course in life. Each of them had formed a more or less shocking and unorthodox liaison which had, in the end, brought her to this place. Yet, and not surprisingly, they did not think of themselves as a little band of sisters. When human beings live in intimacy and isolation, their similarities often disappear from the reckoning. It is their differences that dominate. Mary and Claire were sisters of a kind, of course, but they shared no blood and, as Claire had wistfully noted in her journal, they could find something to fight about every day. It often seemed to them, especially to Mary, that they shared nothing in their

lives except, to their exasperation, each other's lives. For Claire,
Jane was little more than an acquaintance. For Mary, after the
year they had spent keeping company, Jane was more than
that but still not much more. Had the time come, which now
would never come, for the two couples to go their separate
ways there was little behind them to suggest the parting would
have been any great wrench for Mary. After the intense and
revealing hugger-mugger of life at Casa Magni, Jane had seen
Mary at her cold and neurotic worst. Mary had now seen Jane's
flashes of selfishness and vanity from far too close. Jane and
Mary, both, might have been more than ready to accept parting
with equanimity. The next few days were to change all that.
When the little ship foundered, it went down under them,
too. It left Mary, especially, clinging to whatever was left adrift
that might save her. With all the passion that grief and guilt
and desperation could bestow, she seized on two things. The
first was the genius of her dead husband. The wife who had
grown cold now became nothing less than his evangelist, ready
to turn the rest of her life into a passionate martyrdom in his
cause. The second was Jane. They were sisters in grief. They
bore the shock and trial of the uncertain days and the final
terrible and certain facts together, minute by minute, tear by
tear, but the bond lay deeper than that. It lay in the very fact
that Shelley had been swayed by Jane's beauty. Whether Mary
yet knew that Shelley and Jane had been lovers it is impossible
to know. It is certain that she knew of his tenderness for her.
In the first shock of Shelley's death, it seems that she was
impelled, perhaps willed herself – and, above all, needed – to
see Jane as he had seen her. Allowing his feelings for Jane to
be rekindled after his death in her own heart seems to have

been a strange way but a powerful way to repossess him. Mary, of course, had read *Epipsychidion* in manuscript, long before it reached Emily Brontë and transfused some of its lifeblood into *Wuthering Heights*. It takes no great leap of imagination to hear the line in Mary's voice: 'You don't understand. I *am* Shelley.'

There is no question about the strength or the nature of her feeling for Jane, or the fact that it began as a kind of epiphany at the moment of their bereavement. Three years later, Mary would write to Leigh Hunt, 'the hope and consolation of my life is the society of Mrs W. To her, for better or worse, I am wedded.' Two years later than that, her letters to Jane are still peppered with the kind of praises for her beauty that a lover might write. From one of those future letters we gain a telling insight into Mary's state of mind at Casa Magni. Jane's account of her own emotional instability in the autumn of 1827 alarms Mary. 'That dreadful irritability ending in tears which you describe, puts me in mind of my sufferings at Lerici – but I think mine were greater – and they were accompanied by a depression of spirits, beyond anything I had ever felt before, the gloomy shadow of the dark hour whose night still envelops me.' By her 'sufferings' she means the miscarriage. 'Depression of spirits' needs no translation into modern terms and 'dreadful irritability ending in tears' is easily recognised as the classical preface to nervous breakdown. When Shelley left Casa Magni, Mary, spent and weak and in the pit of depression, was on the edge – indeed, leaning well over the edge – of that breakdown. You might have expected the final, fatal blow to precipitate a final, fatal disintegration but she was tougher than she knew. Of all of them, Mary was the one who was already drowning before the shipwreck. She came out of it swimming and swam on with steady purpose for the rest of her life. Becoming 'wedded' to Jane, the sharer of her widowhood, was part of the sea-change. She had been desperate to leave the purgatory of Casa Magni and, yet, she became wedded to that, too. Within days she had quit the physical building for ever but in her way, she never left it.

Ten

On Saturday, the 6th, Williams wrote to Jane.

> I have just left the quay, my dearest girl, and the wind blows right across to Spezzia, which adds to the vexation I feel at being unable to leave this place. For my own part, I should have been with you in all probability on Wednesday evening, but I have been kept day after day, waiting for Shelley's definitive arrangements with Lord B. relative to poor Hunt, whom, in my opinion, he has treated vilely. A letter from Mary, of the most gloomy kind, reached S. yesterday, and this mood of hers aggravated my uneasiness to see you; for I am proud, dear girl, beyond words to express, in the conviction, that wherever we may be together you could be cheerful and contented.

'Gloomy' doesn't quite catch the spirit of that letter from Mary. 'Frantic' might come nearer. Again, she presses Shelley to find a house in Pugnano and tells him that if she doesn't hear from him in the shortest possible time, she is determined to up sticks, quit the nightmare of Casa Magni and come directly to Pisa to force his hand. It is unmistakably a letter from a woman on the edge of breakdown but Williams, the would-be dramatist, finds in it hardly more than a cue for that smug reflection on his own good fortune. Just as revealing, and more telling in hindsight, is the studied glimpse of himself as windswept romantic hero when clearly he knew that, just then, he had been cast as hardly more than a walk-on and left to cool his heels.

Would I could take the present gale by the wings and reach you tonight; hard as it blows, I would venture across for such a reward. However, tomorrow something decisive shall take place; and if I am detained, I shall depart in a felucca, and leave the boat to be brought round in company with Trelawny in the *Bolivar*. He talks of visiting Spezzia again in a few days. I am tired to death of waiting – this is our longest separation, and seems a year to me. Absence alone is enough to make me anxious, and indeed, unhappy; but I think if I had left you in our own house in solitude, I should feel it less than I do now. – What can I do? Poor S. desires that I should return to you, but I know secretly wishes me not to leave him in the lurch. He too, by his manner, is as anxious to see you almost as I could be, but the interests of poor H. keep him here; in fact, with Lord B. it appears they cannot do anything – who actually said as much as that he did not wish his name to be attached to the work, and of course to theirs.

In Lord Byron's family all is confusion; the cut-throats he is so desirous to have about him, have involved him in a second row; and although the present banishment of the Gambas from Tuscany is attributed to the first affair of the dragoon, the continued disturbances among his and their servants is, I am sure, the principal cause for its being carried into immediate effect. Four days (commencing from the day of our arrival in Leghorn) were only given them to find another retreat; and as Lord B. considers this a personal, though tacit attack upon himself, he chooses to follow their fortunes in another country. Genoa was first selected – of that government they could have no hope; Geneva was then proposed, and this proved as bad if not worse. Lucca is now the choice, and Trelawny was despatched last night to feel their way with the governor, to whom he carried letters. All this time Hunt is shuffled off from day to day, and now, heaven knows, when or how it will end . . .

How I long to see you: I had written when, but I will make no promises, for I too well know how distressing it is to both of us to break them. Tuesday evening at furthest, unless kept by the weather, I will say, 'Oh, Jane! how fervently I press you and our little ones to my heart.'

Adieu! – Take body and soul: for you are at once my heaven and earth; that is all I ask of both.

E. ELK. W——

S. is at Pisa, and will write tonight to me.

On Sunday, Hunt went to the Campo Santo like any other tourist and Shelley spent an amiable day as his guide. By Monday, he was satisfied that he had done all he could to put things right between Hunt and Byron and, if he was not altogether convinced that Byron would be as good as his word, he was happy to have got from him a promise to let Hunt have the manuscript of *The Vision of Judgement*, his double-barrelled satire aimed with killing and comic effect at both the poet laureate, Robert Southey, and the lately dead king. This was good stuff for Hunt to get. So good, in fact that it would lead eventually to his being convicted and fined, again, for endangering the peace and calumniating His Late Majesty. But the important thing was that the project was still alive, Byron was still on side and Hunt's journey had not been a tragic waste. It was enough to raise Shelley's spirits. He shopped, he went to the bank, he met their old and good friend Mrs Mason in the street. She thought he looked as happy that morning as she had ever seen him. Before noon, he had left for Livorno by post-chaise. If the day was a little cooler in the port than in the city, it was not by much. The fierce heatwave continued but, by noon, it was clear to some that this day was different from those that had gone before it. It was coming up to the hottest part of the day before they were ready to cast off and the air to seaward was murky and thick. Trelawny had made up his mind to leave harbour in *Bolivar* and keep company with them up the coast but his plan was scuppered. It was his buccaneering disdain for authority that had stored up trouble. The harbour officers, clearly, were only waiting for the next opportunity to slap him down and this was it.

> When we were under weigh, the guard-boat boarded us to overhaul our papers. I had not got my port clearance, the captain of the port having refused to give it to the mate, as I had often gone out without. The officer of the Health Office consequently threatened me with forty days' quarantine. It was hopeless to think of detaining my friends. Williams had been for days fretting and fuming to be off; they had no time to spare, it was past two o'clock, and there was very little wind. Suddenly and reluctantly I re-anchored, furled

my sails, and with a ship's glass watched the progress of my friend's boat.

My Genoese mate observed, 'They should have sailed this morning at three or four a.m., instead of three p.m. They are standing too much in shore; the current will set them there.'

I said, 'They will soon have the land-breeze.'

'Maybe,' continued the mate, 'she will soon have too much breeze; that gaff top-sail is foolish in a boat with no deck and no sailor on board.' Then pointing to the S.W., 'Look at those black lines and the dirty rags hanging on them out of the sky – they are a warning; look at the smoke on the water; the devil is brewing mischief.'

There was a sea-fog, in which Shelley's boat was soon after enveloped, and we saw nothing more of her.

The afternoon's heat was oppressive. Trelawny, like a sensible man, took to his cabin for a siesta. What woke him was the commotion aboard *Bolivar* and other vessels alongside in the harbour, the drum and rattle of chains passing through the hawses as crews laid second anchors and urgently hove all and everything fast and snug before the gale hit. It was soon on them, with a violent wind and rain and thunder. In not much above twenty minutes the storm was over. Trelawny looked through the clearing air to see if he could catch sight of Shelley's boat.

Eleven

I have heard that all this time, Shelley was in brilliant
spirits. Not long before, talking of presentiment, he had
said that the only one he ever found infallible was the
certain advent of some evil fortune when he felt particularly
joyous. Yet, if ever fate whispered of coming disaster, such
inaudible but not unfelt prognostics hovered round us. The
beauty of the place seemed unearthly in its excess: the
distance we were from all signs of civilisation, the sea at our
feet, its murmurs or its roaring for ever in our ears – all
these things led the mind to brood over strange thoughts,
and, lifting it from everyday life, caused it to be familiar
with the unreal. A sort of spell surrounded us; and each
day, as the voyagers did not return, we grew restless and
disquieted, and yet, strange to say, we were not fearful of
the most apparent danger.

Mary Shelley, Notes to the Poems of 1822

The most apparent danger, in the eyes of knowledgeable
observers, as little *Ariel* left Livorno, lay in that spanking suit
of sails. The little yacht had six of them and it seems that
Williams had set them all. There were the two slant triangles
of the jib and staysail at the bow, then a larger, lower sail on
each mast and, higher on each mast, those smaller, detached
upper sails, called gaff topsails, that Trelawny's Genoese mate
had thought they'd be better without. With sails come ropes

to make them work. Each sail has a rope attached, called a halyard, by which its top end is hauled aloft. There were no yards aboard *Ariel* – and they'd be rarer than hens' teeth in any modern yacht marina – but the name of the rope that hoists a sail still recalls the time when sails were square and went up fastened to yards. (Landlubbers always speak of a 'yard-arm' but that, according to Admiral Smyth, is just the the outer quarter or so of a yard.) Six halyards, then, plus an extra two for the outer ends of those gaffs, and all these straining ropes made fast with turns around a cleat or pin somewhere or other around the boat. More ropes: the triangular jib and staysail have each a pair of ropes attached to their one free corner and called, for whatever reason, sheets. When under way with the sail rigged, one sheet will be made fast and will be under tension, taking the strain as the sail is filled out and driven by the wind, while the other sheet lies idle on the windward side. By easing the working sheet out or hauling it harder in, the sailor controls the shape and efficiency of the sail. The large sails on each mast, each fastened by their long foot to a wooden boom, are also provided with sheets, in this case a rather more complicated arrangement that means the same rope is used whichever side the wind blows from.

Sailors of a certain sort seem to breed ropes and it is certainly not beyond the wit of an improving yachtsman, like Williams, to add to this total of twelve ropes, but the round dozen is what had to be handled to get all sail off *Ariel* and keep her naked booms safely under control. (The next sailor to be knocked overboard or killed outright by an unrestrained boom in a rolling sea will be neither the first nor the last but only one of many.)

Shelley's Boat

A dozen ropes, then, and just three pairs of hands – two of those hands being Shelley's. One hand at least would have to be clapped firmly on the tiller at all times. It leaves plenty to do for the remaining available hands, should there be a need to bring the sails down.

And there was.

It may seem odd to mention the three-times-world-champion racing driver Jackie Stewart at this point, but little *Ariel*, in her own way, was a speed machine. That's what Williams liked best about her. Stewart once surprised an interviewer who was asking the usual breathless questions about a racing driver's lightning reactions. 'I don't believe my reactions are any quicker than anybody else's,' he said. 'They are just appropriate reactions.' In fact, he went on to explain, they weren't really reactions at all. They were anticipations. You knew what was going to happen, so you did the appropriate thing before it started to happen. If you left it until you were reacting, then you had left it rather too late.

' . . . they told me on their return . . . that she was a ticklish boat to manage, but had sailed and worked well, and with two good seamen she would do very well; and that they had cautioned the gents accordingly.'

Some caution in a similar spirit should perhaps go along, more often than it does, with the keys of fast cars. In his sports machine of a yacht, Edward Williams was in a position that Jackie Stewart would recognise. In some ways he was better off. There was plenty of time. Hours of it, in fact, for anticipating the inevitable change and no shortage of clues in the sea and sky. In some ways he was worse off. If you've left things until you are reacting instead of anticipating, it takes much more time to interfere with arrangements involving twelve wet ropes, flogging sails and flailing gaffs, on a boat being thrashed about by wind and wave, than it does to twitch a steering wheel or adjust the pressure of your right foot. Much, much more time. Yet, when the moment comes, a 'ticklish' yacht can go disastrously out of control in the same blink of an eye as a speeding car.

All that is certain can be easily said. The thunderstorm blew up and, in it, caught out in their open boat, they were overwhelmed and died.

Much more can, and has been, said about the events and details of the shipwreck. Some of it is reasonable inference and rather more of it is excitable speculation. Some of it counts as wild romance, yet carries off its implausibility so boldly as to have passed almost for fact. Many years later, an old and dying fisherman is said to have confessed, on his deathbed of course, to having been in the crew of a felucca that ran them down in the storm, deliberately and with intent to steal the gold the Milordo Inglese had aboard. It is believable that a simple fisherman might confuse Shelley with Byron, or any Englishman with any other, but no sailor, however simple, could have mistaken Shelley's boat for Byron's. *Ariel* was hardly more than a skiff in comparison to the grandeur of *Bolivar*. Still, any English toff might have been a *milordo* to the deckhand of a felucca and all of them stinking rich. It was a fact that Shelley had fifty pounds aboard, loaned by Byron, that he'd drawn out of the bank that morning, as any lounger might have seen. Had the suppositious lounger passed the word to the quayside? A felucca was said to have followed them out of the harbour. How suspicious might that be? Not very suspicious, given that Livorno was a port and that many feluccas regularly plied up and down to Genoa. Trelawny tells us, when describing his anxious watching hours after the storm, that: 'I watched every speck that loomed on the horizon, thinking that they would have borne up on their return to the port, as all the other boats that had gone out in the same direction had done.'

The traffic, then, amounted to more than *Ariel* and a mysterious skulduggery felucca.

The run-down-by-a-felucca hare was started after Captain Roberts – picking up where Trelawny had left off – salvaged *Ariel* from a hundred and twenty feet or so of water. When she emerged, some of her timbers were found to be stove in. Trelawny tells us that he and Roberts 'and every other sailor' were agreed that this was evidence that she had been run down by a heavier vessel. It seems plausible enough, of course. But it was also convenient. Fell work by a felucca let both of them off any uncomfortable hook of responsibility. These were, after all, the two men in the circle who had most to do with the building of *Ariel* and both knew her to be a boat that could bite. It was Trelawny's style to be sweeping, but here he is a touch too sweeping. Could it be true that in all that numerous body of men called 'every other sailor' there was none to point out that salvage operations, especially from deep water, commonly inflict some damage on the vessels they lift? 'I . . . engaged two large feluccas with drags and tackling,' writes Trelawny, 'to go before, and endeavour to find the place where Shelley's boat had foundered . . . ' Large boats hauling 'drags and tackling' are not exactly a nautical equivalent of tweezers.

Going back to Roberts's reports, we find that in his first letter to Trelawny, there is no mention of damage at all.

> We have got fast hold of Shelley's boat, and she is now safe at anchor off Via Reggio. Everything is in her, and clearly proves that she was not capsized. I think she must have been swamped by a heavy sea; we found in her two trunks, that of Williams containing money and clothes, and Shelley's, filled with books and clothes.
>
> Yours very sincerely,
>
> DAN ROBERTS

No mention of damage at all, only of a boat that when raised and baled out was whole enough to be left riding safely to an anchor. Mention of the damage turns up in another letter, a little later that same month. Roberts lets Trelawny know the results of auctioning the wreck ('a trifle more than two hundred dollars') without bothering to mention that he himself was the buyer. It is only in a postscript that Roberts adds: 'On a close examination of Shelley's boat, we find many of the timbers on the starboard quarter broken, which makes me think for certain, that she must have been run down by some of the feluccas in the squall.'

Would it really take a close examination to spot the damage done to a little yacht that had been smashed into and sunk by a felucca? It wouldn't be every other sailor who would think so. Perhaps the most telling thing is that this remark is a postscript. Other damage is mentioned in the letter – the masts had been carried away, the bowsprit had been broken, a gunwale stove in – but these are mentioned in a matter-of-fact way, as if they were simply to be expected. He also mentions, with no comment, that the hull was half full of blue clay, out of which he fished clothes, books, a spy-glass and other articles. He expresses no surprise at the presence of this blue clay and does not seem to expect any on Trelawny's part. As to its source, he makes no comment. I make the assumption that blue clay is what you'll find the drag will scrape up, if you were to trawl it along the seabed off Viareggio behind a large felucca. Either the sinking *Ariel* scooped blue clay aboard with her own gunwale or it was pushed aboard by the gear that found her lying there. In either case, a certain amount of damage might be taken for granted, as it is in the body of the letter.

The 'run down by a felucca' theory looks too much like the postscript that it is, and too much like a convenient, conscience-saving afterthought between the correspondents. Trelawny knew it was, at the very least, a shaky conclusion. In his own, much later, account – in the manuscript version, anyway – his last word on the subject reads, 'Shelley's boat might have foundered & the damage of her hull done in getting her up – and not by having been run down – ', but, at the time, it was clearly best to stand shoulder to shoulder with Roberts so that neither shoulder should bear any blame. Of course, they weren't to blame. All the same, it was only weeks since Trelawny had seen and told them what an unhandy crew they were, apart from the boy. He'd laughed at them, and Williams had not liked it. He'd given them good advice, too – at least, he tells us that he had – and Williams hadn't taken it.

Shelley's Boat

There was a shadow of dread but perhaps, also, a shadow of guilt lying on Trelawny's heart as he had looked anxiously seaward as the storm-tossed feluccas came in.

> I sent our Genoese mate on board some of the returning crafts to make inquiries, but they all professed not to have seen the English boat . . . During the night it was gusty and showery, and the lightning flashed along the coast; at daylight I returned on board and resumed my examinations of the crews of the various boats which had returned to the port during the night. They either knew nothing or would say nothing. My Genoese, with the quick eye of a sailor, pointed out on board a fishing-boat an English-made oar that he thought he had seen in Shelley's boat, but the entire crew swore by all the saints in the calendar that this was not so.

While a single oar might have been plucked up, guiltily, as flotsam, it is hardly credible loot and, as evidence of piracy, does not even amount to a straw to clutch at.

Captain Roberts told Mary and Jane – this while there was still a shred of hope to cling to – that he had taken his telescope to the top of the harbour's tower and had seen the men aboard *Ariel* ten miles out, off Viareggio, taking in their top'sls. Perhaps it just came out, prompted by an urge he couldn't suppress, a wish to nourish their hopes, despite all appearances. The women, their hearts torn with dread, wanted to believe him. Others may have been more sceptical. Viareggio is not ten miles from the tower at Livorno. It is just about twice that far. Even allowing a generous radius for the term 'off Via Reggio', Roberts was claiming what mariners and aviators call unlimited visibility – ten kilometres or better is the modern formal qualification – but others described something quite different. We have Trelawny saying he lost sight of them in a 'sea-fog' shortly after leaving the port. Trelawny's use of language is loose, but what he reports is something like what you'd expect: in the conditions that breed such a thunderstorm, that would be a thick, milky haze. It isn't technically a fog but, rather, a condition of extreme humidity in which the air holds just about as much water as it is capable of holding in the form of vapour. We talk of fog as a 'vapour' but it isn't that to a physicist or meteorologist. Vapour is invisible, molecular in scale, while fog comes in perfectly visible droplets. As we all know, fog droplets can baffle the passage of light in a matter of inches. Light may travel much more easily through vapour but, still, those water molecules baffle it in the end, bouncing it this way and that way and smearing it all out into the general whiteness that, even in England, is the colour of the horizon on lazy, hazy summer days. If, on one of those lazy, hot, humid days, you were to stand on the top deck of a ferry in Dover harbour, or even on top of a white cliff, you would need a truly remarkable telescope to penetrate the haze and pick out a tiny sailboat just outside Calais. In the much higher humidity of a Mediterranean heatwave to pick out yet more detail at such a distance would be even more astonishing.

No, it is extremely unlikely that Roberts could have seen so much, so far off. But perhaps he wanted to convince himself as much as the widows-elect that he had. It shows uncommon concern for Roberts to have watched them for so long and to have 'gained leave' to climb the tower.

Shelley's Boat

Had he been worried about those top'sls, the crankiness of that boat? Why had he not tried harder to dissuade them from going? There had been, of course, the comforting fact that, as they were getting ready to leave, Trelawny was also preparing to cast off and accompany them at least part of the way. The idea that Trelawny would be at hand in the larger and altogether sounder *Bolivar* must have been a thought to ease his mind. But Trelawny and *Bolivar* had fallen foul of the port authorities and, as we have seen, were prevented from sailing.

After a while, there were those 'who had professed to see' the Englishmen's yacht. Roberts found some fishermen who claimed to have seen it go down. Later, from somewhere, there came the story of a fishing vessel that reported seeing and hailing them just as the storm struck. Nothing could be proved, but Roberts and Trelawny turned the dark brow of suspicion that way. The fishermen's story was that, seeing the little yacht still carrying all her canvas and seemingly unaware of the force about to strike her, they had urged the crew by desperate cries to reduce sail. One man aboard, they said, stood to go about the task but another raised an arm and restrained him, almost, it might have been, angrily. After that, the fishermen said, they were too busy saving themselves to know what became of the pleasure yacht. If they said they had lost sight of it in the welter of the storm, it is easy to believe them. Trelawny and others were content to let the suspicion hang in the air that these men – or others like them – in their reticence were holding back something guilty.

An imaginary counsel for the defence of these fishermen might well rise in court and ask whether it is likely that men who had carried out an act of piracy would report having seen the victim at all? Why should they, when their actions would have been screened from all eyes by no less impenetrable a screen than a violent storm at sea? The same counsel might well bob up to ask whether it is plausible that piratical fishermen, bent on stealing gold, would deliberately plough down an open boat in a raging sea, when a more certain way of losing the gold to Davy Jones could hardly be contrived. It may be, one imagines Captain Roberts saying, with perhaps a little dry-throated cough, that they had meant to come alongside and board *Ariel* and that the ramming was unintentional. Counsel asks Captain Roberts, mildly enough, whether or not sea-room was the sailor's single most important life-saving imperative in such conditions. Captain Roberts agrees that it is. Counsel asks, still mildly, whether it is not true that Captain Roberts and Mr Trelawny and 'every other sailor' all know perfectly well that an attempt to board one boat from another in thrashing waves and a thundering wind would be a most dangerous, and very probably lethal, undertaking and that it is one no sailor, not even a pirate, would be eager to consider in such a storm. Captain Roberts has no answer but to shrug and nod and twist his lips somewhat. The impartial judge asks whether he is to take that as meaning yes. Captain Roberts says that he may. The men who sail Ligurian feluccas, counsel suggests, may or may not be rogues enough when opportunity offers but they know their business aboard a boat in a storm and it is not acts of piracy. It is using their skill and knowledge to save their ship and their souls. Which, of course, they did, so ensuring that they came back to make their report, while Mr Williams and Mr Shelley, most regrettably, did not. Counsel almost sits, but draws himself up again. He has not quite finished with Captain Roberts in the witness box. Is it not true, he asks, that when you first saw the design for this yacht, you expressed some concerns. Captain Roberts agrees that this was so. With some prompting, he admits that he had thought her over-canvassed for her displacement and depth of keel. And yet – counsel fingers certain papers that lie before him – between the 18th and the 22nd of May, at Lerici, you helped the deceased Mr Williams to add extensions to the mast and make certain other modifications in order to carry yet more sail. In a quiet, low voice, Captain Roberts agrees that this was so. And the purpose of these additions? Mr Williams, having tried the yacht against *Bolivar*, was eager to find more speed. Had you changed your original opinion and reservations? No. Then you mean you assisted in the modifications against your better judgement. Yes. And why did you do that? Because Mr Williams would not be gainsaid and I believed that if it were to be done, it were best to be done well and properly. But you must have believed that it made the vessel inherently more dangerous, says counsel, with a puzzled frown. Captain Roberts pauses for a moment before replying. In a deliberate voice, he says that he believed it increased the requirement for skill in handling the vessel. And did Captain Roberts believe that Mr Williams had that skill? Captain Roberts said that, at the time, he hoped and believed that Mr Williams was acquiring that skill. It appears, most sadly, says counsel in a sombre tone, that your hope was a vain one.

Captain Roberts's weather-beaten face assumes an unwonted pallor. The imaginary counsel sits.

Shelley's Boat

Of course, it is still possible that they were run down by a felucca without any piratical intention being involved and possible, too, that the crew of such a felucca may have kept their mouths shut. Certainly, little *Ariel* would have come off much the worse in a collision. Feluccas were vessels distantly related to the Arab dhow, with that same distinctive triangular sail-on-a-big-stick known as a lateen. Or, rather, two of them as the felucca was two-masted. There was no regulation size or weight, of course, for feluccas but, at this time, they were among the trading workhorses of the Mediterranean and accordingly big-timbered. The feluccas Shelley and Williams would have seen tramping up and down the coast off Porto Venere might have been laden with cargoes amounting to four hundred barrels of preserved tuna or five hundred sacks of Indian corn. A commonplace, even small, felucca might be five or six times the weight of *Ariel*.

Finding himself on a collision course with a much smaller vessel in a storm – and in a storm, as in a fog, the discovery may come suddenly and late – the helmsman of a felucca might have hard choices and few. At the time, he would be running before the wind, his greatest anxiety to make sure that he is stern-on to the following seas. A sudden turn might mean the risk of broaching and an experienced helmsman's deepest instinct is to guard against broaching. A mishandled or badly rigged boat running before the wind may be flung by the forces of wind and sea into a turn much more abrupt than any the helm could ever command. Its proper motion suddenly lost, and likely to be laid flat by the wind, the boat then lies at the mercy of the storm-driven wave behind her. In fact, it isn't just the wind that throws the boat flat and ready, in the worst case, to be rolled over. It's physics, too. Inertia keeps the mast and upper parts of the boat going the way they were going before the boat's foot was suddenly twisted broadside-on, like a brake in the water. It is this combination of wind, wave and momentum that makes a broach such a boat-breaking event. Faced with something amounting to a big skiff, the helmsman of our hypothetical felucca might well decide that his best course is to hit determinedly bow-on, making sure that the strength of his heavily timbered stem, always especially massive in a felucca, takes – and delivers – the force of the blow. Better to go right through a small boat than broach and be rolled over her by a storm-driven wave. The little boat, after all, wasn't going to come out either way and what chance would there be of saving anybody? Should he and his felucca survive, the less said about other boats no longer in evidence the better. On the face of it there is much that is plausible in Roberts's and Trelawny's insinuations. Trelawny, anxious to make the case, points out another unhelpful quirk of maritime laws, written and unwritten.

So remorselessly are the quarantine laws enforced in Italy, that, when at sea, if you render assistance to a vessel in distress, or rescue a drowning stranger, on returning to port you are condemned to a long and rigorous quarantine of fourteen or more days. The consequence is, should one vessel see another in peril, or even run it down by accident, she hastens on her course, and by general accord not a word is said or reported on the subject.

Plus ça change. These days, aboard tankers and container

ships, so it is said, the daybreak watch now and then find in mid-ocean that, at some time in the night, they have collected portions of aluminium mast and lengths of yacht rigging on the foredeck. The standard procedure, not written in any handbook, is to cut it away and return it to the water without mention in the log. Report, after all, begets inquiry and inquiries beget blame. They also mean lost time and money and to what good? What can be changed? And so, apart from the splash, the rule is silence. All of this, no doubt, will be denied by the directors of any shipping line in the world, a denial that will make it not a whit less believable. Just as, with or without the hint of piracy, the theory Roberts and Trelawny decided to put about was at least believable, then as now.

But it won't do, mostly because it is so entirely unnecessary, except to two men. In cases like this, men and women who are entirely blameless and who could not possibly have altered the outcome, often do say, 'I blame myself . . . ' Roberts and Trelawny, on the other hand, had real shadows flickering in their consciences. It was not a formula they could use. To escape it, they stood in need of something more elaborate than the mere fact. But that fact is a simple one. To account for the sinking of that boat on that day, one circumstance alone is more than enough: being caught unprepared in a violent squall beneath a thunderhead.

In the last analysis, the most overwhelming evidence against the run-down-by-a-felucca theory was all still neatly in the hull of *Ariel* herself when she was raised. Apart from the three men, and the little ship's tender they had built for getting ashore – it would be found washed ashore near

Viareggio – just about everything that had been stowed aboard when they left Livorno was still aboard. There, still inside the hull, was Shelley's chest with its clothes and books and Williams's with clothes and money. Up came Shelley's notebook and Williams's journal. There were the cases of beer for the Casa Magni larder. There was the little barrel of wine for Maglian, the friendly and helpful harbour master at Lerici. (There had, obviously, been nothing personal in the miscalculation over customs dues.) When an open boat is overturned things fall out. By the time they have descended through twenty fathoms, those things will be spread over a wide swathe of seabed. All *Ariel*'s things went down, all the way, inside the boat. It follows that she did not overturn but went to the bottom upright. This is liklely enough. She was, in Trelawny's sailor-like vocabulary, 'crank', which Admiral Smyth has defined for us as meaning 'a vessel, by her construction or her stowage, inclined to lean over a great deal . . . ' Suddenly they were caught in a more violent and turbulent wind than any they had ever met, and in a welter of angry waves, little, open, undecked *Ariel* would have leaned her gunwale into the green water like the lip of a spoon. Had she broached, she would simply have scooped her way underwater. She would have filled in a moment with the next swamping wave.

Other things have been read into what passed for eye-witness reports. Let us go back to the little vignette reported by the fishermen. One man aboard, they said, stood to go about the task but another raised an arm and restrained him, almost, it might have been, angrily. There are readers who, in a kind of romantic wish-fulfilment, see in this the figure of

Shelley's Boat

Williams about to take in sail, while Shelley, more than half in love with death and sick of life, his giant romantic soul enthralled by this glorious intimacy with the forces of nature, forcefully prevents him, so ensuring that they will die or, at least, roll the dice with indifference. Shelley, after all, left behind him, unfinished, *The Triumph of Life*, with its shocking sense of life itself as a kind of tyranny, brutally indifferent to the fate, suffering or identity of individuals. He was aware of his public failure as a poet. He had, perhaps, just grown old enough to realise his failure as a father. His wife had just miscarried and nearly died and, while he had saved her, he was far from sure their marriage was saveable. True, he had written of his bliss, living on the edge of that beautiful bay, and that he could wish the day to last for ever. On that last day when he left Pisa, his friend Mrs Mason even thought he looked as well and happy as she had ever known him. Yet death was on his mind. He had asked Trelawny to see about getting him that supply of prussic acid, so as to have about him the means, etc . . . Beyond all this there are the constant references in his poetry to death by drowning, to mystical translations at sea, boats that bear their sailors beyond the bounds of life. Here he was, by fatal chance, living the last stanzas of his own *Adonais*. He embraced the storm and all it meant. It makes biographical and literary sense.

But not common sense. Shelley may have been half in love with easeful death, but there's not a syllable to say that Williams was. There is much that says Williams was in love with life. It was his eagerness, expressed so frankly, naïvely and – given the circumstances – so touchingly in the last letter from Livorno, to be with Jane again, as soon as may be, that made him so little inclined to heed the voices that bade him wait out the weather. Shelley was ready to take the advice, but in sea-matters he did not make his own decisions. Williams was master there and Williams was not a man to heed the advice of others. He did not want to die, he just wanted to be home. His estimate to Trelawny was that if they got off the quayside by noon, they would be home by seven. One imagines him making the calculation. Good time for a meal, some wine, some talk, a little yawning and an early retreat to bed with Jane after kicking his heels and sleeping alone for a week in Livorno. He was seaman enough, he believed, to trust his own judgement when it came to weather and his command was to set sail.

How would it have come about that Shelley suddenly and fatally took command? Why would Williams, in a crisis, have tamely accepted this sudden and improbable demotion? It requires a sudden change of character in each of them.

What does not require any change of character is an explanation in which Williams demonstrates that he is not the kind of man to be told. He wouldn't be told that his design was less than perfect. He wouldn't be – indignantly wouldn't be – told by Trelawny that it would be a good idea to hire a couple of locally knowledgeable Ligurian sailors. He wouldn't be told about the habits of the local weather by locals if their opinion differed from his own. He wouldn't be told that it was a bad idea to set out from Livorno with a thunderstorm brewing. How, then, was he likely to respond when told that it was time to take in sail by a bunch of paltry rascals in a fishing boat? He was probably offended that men of their rank should have the temerity even to address him with their opinions. Vivian, of course, knew perfectly well that the fishermen were right and it was surely Vivian who leapt up to hand the top'sls. That, after all, would have been his job. It certainly wouldn't have been Shelley's. It is entirely in character for Williams verbally and physically to thrust him back and, probably, to curse him for his indiscipline. Wait for my order. It is altogether in character for Williams to have made him wait for the word of command. And, just to show him – and those ignorant, offensive fishermen – who was in charge, it might have seemed a good thing to make him wait all the longer for it. Wait for my order. He, Williams, was the man to judge the moment for taking sail. Except that he wasn't and it was entirely in character that, in these circumstances, he would die. If they waited for his order, it would come too late. Williams had now left the territory of 'anticipating'. He was well into that penumbral area on the edge of disaster called 'reacting'.

'For want of a nail . . . ' The nail was, perhaps, that business of getting clearance from the Jack-in-office in the harbour master's tower, that little formality that Trelawny had been in the habit of disregarding. Had Jack-in-office not decided to pin him to the quay, just to teach him a lesson, Trelawny would have sailed out with them. He and *Bolivar* would have met the storm, too, but he and *Bolivar*, seaworthy as any felucca, would have ridden it out. Maybe, just maybe, it would all have been different. Had Williams seen *Bolivar* shortening sail to three reefs and storm jib – or with every stitch of canvas removed – running under bare poles, as sailors say – perhaps he'd have taken a hint that he wouldn't take from a felucca. The captain of one of the feluccas hired

Shelley's Boat

by Trelawny to search 'with drags and tackling' for Shelley's boat had claimed that he had been out in the squall and had seen her founder with every sail still set. There seems good reason to believe him. After all, finding a small hull in twenty fathoms is strong evidence that he knew just where to look.

Perhaps, in any case, they might still have been swamped, but *Bolivar* could have worked down to pick them up, even in that sea. It would have been a proof-test of real seamanship and, more than that, of the courage and the love of a true friend. It would have been magnificent. It would have made a marvellous story. It was, on all grounds, exactly what Trelawny would have tried to do. He'd have been positioned to do it, too, because there is no question but that he would have been wise enough to keep the little yacht under his lee. One wonders how many times in his life Trelawny went through versions of this scenario in his private thoughts, posing the possible combinations of difficulties, the possible seamanlike answers. He must certainly have gone through it that July. Whether or not that little piece of paperwork was the nail that cost Shelley his life, it had certainly cost Trelawny the chance of glory, a chance on which it is easy to believe he would have been ready to risk his life. To have sailed into the heart of a storm and plucked the poet he loved so well from the jaws of death would have made up for missing Trafalgar. Many thousands could speak of the part they had played in saving England. Only one man could have saved Shelley. It would even have had the Nelson touch. Trelawny, eight years a midshipman, would certainly have known the famous story. Nelson, escaping from an overwhelmingly superior enemy squadron, found that Hardy had been left stranded in a small boat between him and the chasing Frenchmen. 'Damn, it,' he had cried, 'I'll not lose Hardy!' and, hauling his ship about, sailed back and plucked up, almost from under the startled enemy's bows, the friend whose parting kiss, when the time came, would be the last tenderness he would know on earth. On that day of glory that Trelawny had just missed. Again, glory had been in the offing and, again, quite literally, Trelawny had just missed the boat.

Twelve

We are free to imagine the final scene of the last act of the drama. After a couple of hours of sluggish progress a fluky wind has started to get up. *Ariel* begins to pick up her heels. Like Williams, Vivian is looking up at the masthead burgee, the little pennant that a yacht holds up to read the wind, as a walker holds up a licked finger. Williams wears a look of sailorly satisfaction to see that the burgee has, at last, grown lively. Vivian notes the sudden flicks that show, moment by moment, abrupt changes of quarter in the rising gusts and there is not much satisfaction in the look he wears. Williams is at the tiller, leaning back into the wind on the weather gunwale, as they all are, to gain the leverage of their weight. Williams is reading the leach of the sail with his eye and feeling the pulse of the tiller in his hand, exhilarated by the surge of pace he is getting out of the boat as the gusts come. The water speeds creamily now away from the lee rail. Under the thickening sky the taut sails no longer cast a shadow, only a deeper gloom on the waves. Then, in a trough, all at once, the little boat picks her dipped gunwale out of the wave and stands up, the full gallop suddenly lost, as Williams the cavalry officer feels it, as if she were a mare about to refuse a hedge. She shakes her sails as if in doubt. A great and loud rippling troubles the mizzen. The gaff jumps as if, for a moment, it had no weight and then the sail seems to catch hold of it again. Vivian has already ducked his head out of

153

the way of the great boom that will lash, murderously, across the boat should Williams allow her to gybe, letting the wind cross her stern and taking her, all unprepared, from the other side. He can see only timber as he feels the yacht heaved by the wave that passes under her. It is not his place to shout 'down helm!' to Mr Williams. It is not his place to shout a warning to Mr Shelley. But Williams does push the helm down and Vivian feels the boat lean to her work once again, on the same tack, with a firm crack of the sail.

Vivian unfolds himself, sits back against the weather rail and looks up at the now dark centre of the sky overhead.

Shelley, to whom Vivian is always more visible than he is to Williams, sees the pale cheek and tries to read his look. He has long since folded his Keats so as to keep his place and thrust the book into his pocket. He has never before needed to shield his companionable book from the lash of salt spray. Then, he has never before felt the little boat leaping beneath them the way it does now in this vigorous sea. *Ariel* – she is definitely *Ariel* now – has never seemed more frail, nor native elements of air and water more full of grandeur. He cannot but feel something exulting within him that they should be so adventured. Of course there is fear, but he has always known that nothing is sublime without fear. He is content to abandon himself to the sublime as Williams seems content to abandon himself to the adventure, as he would to the headlong rush of a cavalry charge. Vivian, he sees, seems not to share in any emotion of this kind. He looks white and troubled. Vivian catches a sense that Shelley is looking at him and returns his glance. Then he looks at the sails, turning his head in a deliberate motion from the mizzen boom to the bow where both jib and staysail are still hard with wind, flying down towards the green of the next wave.

Shelley touches Williams on the arm.

'Williams, do you think it may be time to take a rag or two off her?'

Out of the corner of his eye, Williams sees a little urgent movement in Vivian, readying himself to leap into action at the sheets and halyards, but he gives him no command. There's a little flush of satisfaction in it for Williams, in knowing that the others are beginning to show faint heart.

'Well, well, Shelley. And I thought you were eager to get home.'

'Never a man more so.'

'Then here's the wind, at last, to speed you, and all you do is to complain of it.'

'No complaints, if you have none.'

'The brisker the better, say I. And the sooner to bring a man to the sight and the warm side of the woman he loves.' Williams lowers his eyes briefly from the burgee and catches Shelley in his gaze with a curious smile. 'Though your philosophy, I know, was never confined to a unity in these matters. I should rather say, women.'

Shelley's mouth sets in a pursed smile and he half closes his eyes, either in acknowledgement or because a lash of spray is just then flung back over the weather side from the pitching bow. The sea that had been peculiarly calm is now, of a sudden, surging and restless.

'It would be enough to the purpose to speak of only one.'

'And she so rare,' answers Williams, 'that a poet could do

no other than adore her. I'm not ashamed to say I cannot hold a candle to the poet, for who's the poet that can? But I'll give no man the title of a truer heart than mine, or truer lover. Not you nor any man.'

'She is rare, Williams, and so must you be to be worthy of her.'

Williams claps a hand briefly on Shelley's shoulder and laughs. 'So who would douse the sails that speed him to my Jane? There's a fellow I could pity.'

'Then, come winds and crack your cheeks,' says Shelley.

Another lash of sharp silver spray makes both of them turn their heads away. Vivian barely seems to notice it. He is staring hard to windward where he sees the darkness of rain. The sea hisses away under the lee rail. Williams glances away where Vivian is looking.

'I dare say we're in for a soaking. Well, let he who loves her least give the word to shorten sail. For my part I would not clip my wings a minute sooner than I might.'

Shelley laughs aloud.

'It is hardly wise in you, Williams, to engage me in that way. You know I have had much more practice in drowning than you.'

'But I have not let you do it yet.'

The poet and the helmsman both laugh. Nothing in their manner invites the crewman Vivian to join them. He hears the odd, off-key excitement that has seized them both and Williams in particular. There is too much bravado in it for his liking. He has heard the references to drowning in their conversation and is not inclined to join them in their amusement. He has heard the rest, too, if only in snatches.

Shelley's Boat

He wonders whether the confident Mr Williams knows that Mr Shelley has enjoyed his wife.

Yes. In the wood behind the house, according to Tita. While Mr Shelley's wife was abed recovering from her affliction. While her sister was nursing her in that bedroom at the front of the house. While Mr Williams was playing the shipwright at Lerici, staying away from women's troubles for all the hours he could. Tita assured him that it was easy to see when a man and a woman had known union of the body, even in a drawing-room amidst every politeness. The signs, once you knew them, were clear and in the present case, unmistakable. Out on the terrace, certainly, when he waited on them and the Lady Jane was singing and the others listening under the night sky, it would have been clear to him, even had he not seen them abscond to the wood with his own eyes. A blameless scene, all things as they should be, yet the plain fact that Mr Shelley, an hour or two before, had lain as close to her breast as she now held that guitar might as well have been written on the tablecloth, duly signed by a notary. What were the signs? A whole language of signs. A language the English – Tita says this laughing – ought to know well. Tita believes it is much in vogue amongst English married ladies, having fulfilled all duties to their husbands, to please their husband's friend and themselves also. Vivian has told him he thinks this is not true, but Tita says that every servant in Florence, or Pisa, where there are many English, knows the truth of this. It is the English way. It was the same with the great Lord Nelson in Naples and the Lady Hamilton, as everybody knew. Likewise Captain Trelawny, who receives the same kindness, according to his excellent and intelligent manservant aboard *Bolivar*, from Mrs Wright, whom Vivian would know of. *Si*. Yes, Mrs Wright whose husband made the little ships for Lord Byron and Mr Shelley.

Vivian wonders whether what Tita says he knows is true. More to the point, he wonders whether Mr Williams thinks, or suspects, it true. It crosses his mind to wonder whether Mr Williams's recklessness is goaded by jealousy and this is not a comforting thought.

They become aware of a voice, high and harsh, sounding through the wind and the slap of the waves. A cable away is a felucca, with her boom lowered and lashed to the deck. It is not easy to make out the words they are shouting but Vivian knows what they are saying and their gestures, anyway, make it clear. They are saying, take in sail. When he moves toward the fife rail and the halyards, he feels Williams grasp his arm angrily.

'Boy! I gave you no command.'

The words are drowned by a mighty clap of thunder.

*   *   *

The bodies were washed up at three points, widely separated. Williams came ashore near the mouth of the Serchio, while Shelley's corpse was found five miles or so farther north on the sands of Viareggio. Poor Charles Vivian, in the blue-and-white-striped sailor's trousers and cotton jacket that were probably the extent of his wardrobe, was found later at Massa, farther northwards again. Shelley was still clad as he had been when leaving the quay at Livorno, complete with double-breasted jacket and with his boots and white silks socks still firmly on. Being no swimmer, he might have had no impulse at all to rid himself of the dragging weight of waterlogged clothes, but Williams, so Trelawny thought, had tried to strip in order to swim for his life. All the same, he still had one boot on. It suggests that they had foundered with a suddenness that had caught them out entirely. The clothes at least made them easy to identify. The more they had stripped off, the harder it would have been. The fish, or other things, had eaten most of the flesh that was exposed. Still, there could be no mistake about Shelley. Had there been no other evidence, the copy of Keats's poems, the volume that included *Hyperion* that he had just borrowed from Hunt, folded back as if to keep the place and thrust into a pocket, would have put the matter beyond doubt. In another pocket was a small edition of Sophocles.

*   *   *

As I stood on the threshold of their house, the bearer, or rather confirmer, of news which would rack every fibre of their quivering frames to the utmost, I paused, and, looking at the sea, my memory reverted to our joyous parting only a few days before.

The two families, then, had all been in the verandah overlooking a sea so clear and calm that every star was reflected on the water, as if it had been a mirror; the young mothers singing some merry tune, with the accompaniment of a guitar. Shelley's shrill laugh – I heard it still – rang in my ears, with Williams's friendly hail, the general *buona notte* of all the joyous party, and the earnest entreaty to me to return as soon as possible, and not to forget the commissions they had severally given me. I was in a small boat beneath them, slowly rowing myself on board the *Bolivar*, at anchor in the bay, loath to part from what I verily believed to have been at that time the most united, and happiest, set of human beings in the whole world.

*   *   *

Of course, Trelawny is writing many years afterwards – his *Recollections of the Last Days of Byron and Shelley* was published in 1858, thirty-six years after these events – but it is not the passage of time that has blurred his recall. The old Trelawny style and that vivid sense of telling detail show that his gift for telling a tale is undimmed. As he recalls that moment before the door of Casa Magni, he is not going to let one unfortunate fact get in the way of a good story. He wants to paint the rosy picture of fond memory before going on to – and rather letting himself down with – a platitude. 'And now by the blow of an idle puff of wind the scene was changed. Such is human happiness.'

Trelawny knew perfectly well that the little group at Casa Magni was not 'the most united, and happiest, set of human beings in the whole world'. The truth was that Mary, no negligible member of that set of human beings, was miserable to the point of despair. Nobody at Casa Magni could have failed to know as much and others beyond the hills knew, too. Maria Gisborne knew from Mary's letters from San Terenzo, the first of them back at the beginning of June.

As only one house was to be found habitable in this gulph, the W's have taken up their abode with us, and their servants and mine quarrel like cats and dogs; and besides, you may imagine how ill a large family agrees with my laziness, when accounts and domestic concerns come to be talked of. *Ma Pazienza* – after all, the place does not please me – the people are *rozzi*, and speak a detestable dialect – and yet it is better than any other Italian sea-shore north of Naples – the air is excellent, and you may guess how much better we like it than Leghorn, where besides we should have been involved in English society, a thing we longed to get rid of at Pisa.

Rozzi means boorish or uncouth but using the Italian – and going on to admit the quality of the air – makes her opinion seem more measured than in fact it was.

Two months later, with Shelley dead and Casa Magni fled, there is no longer a restraining urge to dilute the truth:

I described to you the place we were living in: – Our desolate house, the beauty yet strangeness of the scenery and the delight Shelley took in all this – he never was in better health or spirits than during this time. I was not well in body or mind. My nerves were wound up to the utmost irritation, and the sense of misfortune hung over my spirits. No words can tell you how I hated our house and the country about it. Shelley reproached me for this – his health was good and the place was quite after his own heart – What could I answer – that the people were wild and hateful, that though the country was beautiful yet I liked a more countryfied place, that there was great difficulty in living – that all our Tuscans would leave us, & that the very jargon of these Genovese was disgusting –

Shelley's Boat

This was all I had to say but no words could describe my feelings – the beauty of the woods made me weep and shudder – so vehement was my feeling of dislike that I used to rejoice when the winds and waves permitted me to go out in the boat so that I was not obliged to take my usual walk among tree-shaded paths, alleys of vine-festooned trees – all that before I doted on – & that now weighed on me. My only moments of peace were aboard that unhappy boat, when lying down with my head on his knee I shut my eyes & felt the wind & our swift motion alone.

'My ill health might account for much of this,' says Mary. It takes no great wit to suggest that all of this is more likely to have accounted for her ill-health.

It is true that Trelawny may not have known the perfect depth of Mary's misery, for the good reason that, when he was near, her spirits probably improved. All the same, he knew that there were times when, quite simply, she had hated it. He certainly knew that, even before the miscarriage, she had wanted to leave San Terenzo and, after it, wished more strongly than ever. Her insistence that Shelley should look again for a house at Pugnano was among the last of all the words that passed between them.

Trelawny is not publishing a journal and so does not give us a date to go with this picture of the party on the verandah waving him off across the starlit sea with their cheerful *buona notte*. He tells us that it was 'a few days before . . . ' but that is a little bit of cheating in the narrative. The day he had stood outside the door with the heavy news was Friday the 19th of July. His few days would have to be at least a month. Given that he was rowing out to *Bolivar*, the likely date of the 'joyous' evening would be Thursday the 13th of June, the day when, at nine o'clock on a bright morning, he and Roberts had come through the straits of Porto Venere with Byron's little ship, brand new out of the yard, *en route* to Livorno, to pay a cheerful call on the Casa Magni party. It was the day Shelley and Williams tried a little race with her. The vignette could hardly come from a date later than that visit because, on the following Sunday, Mary had her miscarriage and nearly died, which would certainly have altered the mood of Trelawny's little group on the terrace. In fact, it was a week earlier that the miscarriage had first threatened. Through all that week, as Mary told Maria Gisborne in a long letter from the depths a month later, she was 'in great ill health'. She was ill, then, before Trelawny arrived. She was close to dying three days afterwards. She was only just ready to stagger up from her bed a fortnight later, on the day that Shelley and Williams left Casa Magni for the last time. It is hard to know quite when, during those last weeks of Shelley's life, Mary could have been quite such a trouper as to take her place convincingly among 'the happiest people in the world'.

Shelley was much happier with their primitive sea-side life than Mary but, even so, Trelawny well knew that he was no blithe spirit at this time. The scene Trelawny recalls and repaints must have been on the occasion of that maiden-voyage visit from *Bolivar*, and it was then that he and Shelley had their conversation about death and talked of ways of easing oneself out of the world. They had spoken of the comfort to be gained from the possession of prussic acid, 'that golden key to the chamber of perpetual rest'. It is possible to have a conversation about death and about ways of meeting it without speaking from the depths of depression. It is probably a common enough dinner-table topic. But having that conversation with a friend who asks you, on the morrow, to provide him with the chosen means of suicide might exclude him from your list of 'happiest human beings in the world'.

Trelawny is, of course, doing for their lives what he had done for his own. He is painting things as they ought to have been. The truth is in the few searing, desperate lines that Mary scribbled to Leigh Hunt the night before Shelley sailed off to meet him. They hardly make a letter so much as a short, loud scream. She put it in Shelley's hand to deliver:

My Dear friend,

I know that S has some idea of persuading you to come here. I am too ill to write the reasonings only let me entreat you let no persuasions induce you to come, selfish feelings you may be sure do not dictate me – but it would be complete madness to come –

I wish I could write more – I wish I were with you to assist you – I wish I could break my chains and leave this dungeon. – adieu – I shall [. . .] about you & Marianne's health from S –

Your Fn

M.

Be careful, they say, what you wish for. Mary's chains were about to be broken.

Monday's storm had darkened the skies over Lerici, too. If anything, the winds had been worse with them and they assumed that the men would not have sailed. As the week drew to a close they had grown anxious to hear word, but it was not until Friday, when there came a letter from a worried Hunt, begging Shelley to send word of his safe arrival, that they knew for certain that the men had sailed on Monday and had vanished into the storm.

Mary and Jane left at once for Pisa. They arrived at midnight and found Byron but he could tell them nothing they did not already know. Immediately they pressed on to Livorno, where, next day, Roberts encouraged them in delusive hopes. They might have run before the storm, they might have been carried to the coast of Elba or Corsica. At last they came back to Casa Magni. Trelawny went off to scour the coast leaving Claire with instructions to open his post. He must have more than half expected the letter that came from Roberts, that Claire opened. No delusive hopes now. Two bodies had been found. These would prove to be Williams and Vivian. Claire could not bring herself to pass these tidings to the other women. By now, though, Trelawny had been shown the third body, the one that came with a copy of Keats in its pocket, and was on his tireless way to San Terenzo with his certain knowledge of what the sea had yielded up. According to him, no word was necessary. He arrived. They saw him. They knew. According to Mary it was different: ' . . . he launched forth into as it were an overflowing and eloquent praise of my divine Shelley – until I was almost happy that I was thus unhappy to be fed by the praise of him, and to dwell in the eulogy that his loss thus drew forth from his friend.'

One wonders, though, what he had to say to Jane.

Thirteen

What followed was a case of a man rising to the occasion. Rising, indeed, and then soaring beyond what you might call reasonable expectation. Trelawny rose now to create the tallest yet truest tale of his life and his style was to be Homeric. It is time for a closer look at the man.

He was tall, six feet or more, in an age when Byron's five foot eight could be called 'middle height'. He was dark and no allowances had to be made to call him handsome. 'A kind of half-Arab Englishman' Mary called him with no intention of slighting either Arabs or Cornishmen. She was taken with his 'raven black hair which curls thickly and shortly like a More, dark gray – expressive eyes – overhanging brows, upturned lips and a smile that expresses good nature and kindheartedness'. He arrived, in January of 1822, when she had grown frigid to Shelley, as she had told her journal and as Shelley had told Edward and Jane in verse. At any time, those who knew her thought of Mary as emotionally controlled and unimpulsive. She had now begun to fear that she was a sexual and emotional cripple. The surge that she felt the moment she set eyes on Trelawny must have been, among other things, a sweet relief. 'He recounts the adventures of his youth as eloquently and well as the . . . Greek,' she said. 'He interests my imagination.' And not just her imagination. 'His company is delightful for he excites me to think and if any evil shade the intercourse, time will tell.'

Shelley's Boat

She was more than a little smitten.

Born the same year as Shelley, younger son of a younger son and not much loved, he'd been sent to sea at what was, paradoxically, not a good time to begin a naval career. After Trafalgar, the battle whose glorious hem Trelawny had touched, Napoleon abandoned in disgust any plan that depended on his own or anybody else's navy. If it was blue on the map, or surrounded by blue, he simply conceded it to Britain and looked elsewhere. While this was not good news for Russia, career officers in the Royal Navy would gradually realise over the coming decades that it was bad news for them, too. Especially if they were well down the pecking-order. Nelson had disposed of the naval threat to England and, with it, as the bean-counters of the Treasury would increasingly recognise, the need to keep up that most costly thing, the Nelsonian navy. The year Napoleon stood before Moscow, Trelawny came home from Java, still a midshipman, destined never to be a lieutenant, and still recovering from wounds picked up in an amphibious attack. Things carried on downhill. He married. His family didn't care for the match and neither, it seems, did his young wife. She left him after four years for a military man twice his age.

This summary of Trelawny's past may be described as covering the facts but as far as Trelawny was concerned, facts such as these were banalities best discarded. He seems to have decided that all this was simply not up to being the truth about the Trelawny he knew himself to be. The truth was the beautiful, adventurous, wonderfully improbable tale he had invented to replace all that. The faithless, fugitive, English wife, for instance, vanished from the record. An

167

Shelley's Boat

Oriental child-bride, acquired in an interlude of headlong adventure, took her place. He may have made a voyage to India, following his English wife's desertion, aboard what he calls a 'king's ship', but more likely, if at all, it was a ship of the East India Company's. In his rewrite, these travels became a swashbuckling romance to rival anything in Byron, at the shrine of whose imagination, it must be said, Trelawny's fancy owed a candle or two. Anyway, Keats had helpfully declared that beauty is truth, truth beauty, and that is all ye need to know. In this sense, Trelawny's beautiful version of his own life might well be looked on as his own Romantic work of art and therefore, by Keats's rule, quite as true as it needs to be. If what he had done before turning up in Pisa was mostly remarkable invention, what he was to do later, in the Byronic adventure of the War of Greek Independence, would be even more remarkable, more heroic and, even more improbably, mostly fact. He was even to find himself a child bride. Yet, were it not for this high moment that lay before him now on the Ligurian sands, all these things would have been but noises off in the Romantic drama. With what he was about to do, he became something more than an extra. By his actions now he was to take his place among the dramatis personae.

It began, not promisingly, with a legal impediment. There were sanitary laws in Tuscany and sanitary guards to patrol the coast. It was a sanitary guard who'd been with Trelawny when he'd identified Shelley, though the sanitary guard might not have been as ready as he to go through the dead man's pockets. In fact, that was something the guard should have prevented him from doing. Having done it, he should, strictly speaking, have been put in quarantine. Nobody knew how plagues began and bodies washed up from the sea were held to be deeply suspect in this regard. The law required that they be buried just where they came ashore. The law and the sanitary guards were unyielding, so graves were dug in the sand and the bodies interred. To speed their dissolution, they were covered in quicklime before the sand was thrown back over them. Trelawny planted stakes to mark the position. All this was not, of course, what the widows had wished. Mary wanted Shelley to lie in Rome by his dead son. Jane wanted Williams taken home to England. The authorities were unmoved and, as far as they were concerned, the bodies should also be unmoved, in accordance with the laws for the prevention of disease.

Trelawny suggested 'the ancient custom of burning and reducing the body to ashes'. The idea may have been suggested to him by the practices of the burning ghats of Hindu India, customs with which he and Edward Williams were acquainted. The widows agreed. The authorities were shocked. There was no precedent for such a procedure. Permission to burn bodies on a beach would be still, surely, an unorthodox and shocking request were it to be made today, even though we are well used to cremation as a principle and as a convenient and hygienic practice. Not that we have been used to it for all that long. When the Queen's Surgeon, Sir Henry Thompson, formed the Cremation Society in the 1870s, he had the support of Anthony Trollope and Henry Millais, among others, but he met implacable opposition from both the Home Secretary and the Church. It was a heathen thing, a pagan practice. Certainly it had been done in ancient Greece and Rome but Christianity had come to Rome and done away with it in favour of decent burial, in a grave, where the body might piously await the last day and the resurrection of the flesh. There was some fear that God would be altogether baffled if all he might find was ash. In the 1880s a Welshman was prosecuted for cremating his infant. The court, however, found that his act was not illegal, provided that no nuisance had been caused. The first law to regulate cremation did not arrive until 1902 but it was another fifty years before the law had much in the way of common practice to regulate. Almost every crematorium in Britain dates from later than the Second World War. The Church may nowadays have come to the conclusion that God will not, after all, be frustrated by the ash problem, but in Catholic Italy in 1822 the old orthodoxy held sway. The authorities were opposed to Trelawny's suggestion with a shudder of both instinct and piety.

Of course, it was the ancient, classical, pagan nature of the thing that so strongly recommended it. Trelawny and Mary could be sure that Shelley would have approved heartily. Trelawny turned to the British Minister at Florence. Mr Dawkins had become used to making discreet interventions concerning the brawls, the criminal charges and political transgressions of Byron's circle over the last few months. No doubt he found this more solemn request stranger but less troublesome. It is certain that he brought some diplomatic skill to bear. An order was sent to the Governor of Viareggio, ' . . . to deliver up the remains of Mr Shelley . . . ' The authorities probably took into consideration that the dead were, after all, Protestants. They were going to burn for ever anyway.

Trelawny took it all in hand. He had a blacksmith fashion a kind of furnace, on a portable stand, in which a body might lie to be consumed by fire. He set it up on the sands near the mouth of the Serchio and built the pyre beneath it. He brought frankincense, salt, wine and oil to throw into the flames because, he says, such was the ritual usage of the ancient Greeks. It may be that India, too, had taught him about the stench of burning flesh and the benefit of making practical provisions for it. But frankincense? In all accounts of the cremation – and Trelawny himself left no fewer than ten – frankincense is mentioned in the same breath with the oil and wine. Oil and wine were, then as now, to be had in any village or, indeed, practically any house in Italy. But frankincense? Where would the frankincense shop have been? Frankincense is a resinous gum gained from trees of the genus *Boswellia*, says my dictionary. I had to look it up to find out just what kind of stuff frankincense might be, even though its smell, burning as incense, is a Proustian key that can take me back as far as being a babe in arms, a Catholic child in a Catholic church. It is odd to think that for his pagan ceremony, such a shocking idea to true believers, Trelawny must have turned to the only holders of any competent supply, the local church. Perhaps he made his request at the sacristy of the glorious Cathedral of the Campo Santo. Odder still to think that no one in the church of true believers will have thought it odd that they should be the only modern users of the ancient pagan goods for the worship of the ancient pagan gods.

So, with his frankincense to hand, on the 5th of August, Trelawny exhumed and burned the body of Edward Williams on the beach near Torre di Migliarino, watched by a large and curious crowd.

There was no shortage of spectators the following day, either, at Viareggio when, with the same provisions made ready, he had Shelley's body brought from the grave in the sand. It took a little finding, despite the stakes he had placed. The squad of workers from the sanitary department had dug a long trench before the sound, unmistakable in the circumstances, of the mattock meeting a skull told them they had found the poet. The law imposed quarantine on anybody who should touch the corpse and so the workers had an array of iron forceps and other instruments for grasping it. Moving the body, therefore, was not an over-delicate operation. At least Shelley's body stayed together. The body of Williams, the day before, had been so badly eaten away that the limbs had come away in their tongs at the first pull. He was put into the furnace in lumps.

After more than two weeks steeping in his temporary grave, Shelley's flesh had turned a deep and ghastly indigo. It was the quick-lime, deeply penetrating the tissues. In this lime lay the unexpected secret, the chemistry – alchemy in its way – that touched Trelawny's ritual with the final perfecting stroke of mythic magic.

Drowning in a shipwreck may have been neatly metaphorical for a man always determined to pursue his art and his ideals, come what may, in a world of contrary tides and cruel winds, but as a closing metaphor it had shortcomings. After all, the battle with the sea and storm was not a necessary battle, only a foolish one, ill-judged and ill-managed. These are not things you want in your last metaphor as a poet.

Shelley's Boat

Complete disappearance at sea, vanishing into elemental one-ness, might have made up for much of that, but if you drown off the coast you get washed up on to it as unsavoury flotsam. This is not how the greatest lyric poet of the English language should be last remembered. Trelawny's ritual would, at the least, save Shelley's end from much of that. He saved him, too, from whatever is the fate of ghoulish knick-knacks when Byron asked that the skull should be preserved for him. Byron already had a skull on his desk. He sometimes showily used it as a drinking cup and Trelawny knew where his duty lay. He burned the skull with the rest of Shelley.

With the decision to burn, Trelawny had thought to give his friend a fitting and worthy end. With the accident of all that lime, he achieved a kind of final redeeming transfiguration that he had not foreseen. Before electricity changed things, the brightest light you could get in the theatre came from the burning of lime. The most powerful theatre lights, used to follow the star performer about the stage and usually called 'spotlights' by the audience, are still called 'limes' in the business. Those who saw Shelley's body consumed were awed by the brilliance of his burning. It was a radiance of sublime purity, incandescent, and so intense that it far outshone the brilliance of the Mediterranean afternoon.

Fourteen

Pisa, August 27, 1822
. . . We have been burning the bodies of Shelley and
Williams on the sea-shore, to render them fit for removal
and regular interment. You can have no idea what an
extraordinary effect such a funeral pile has, on a desolate
shore, with mountains in the back-ground and the sea
before, and the singular appearance the salt and frankincense gave to the flame. All of Shelley was consumed,
except his *heart*, which would not take the flame, and is
now preserved in spirits of wine . . .

This was Byron writing to his friend Thomas Moore. He does
not mention that part of the 'extraordinary effect' of the funeral
pile was to make him feel sick, or that he detached himself
from the scene by taking a long, cleansing swim out to the
anchored *Bolivar*. Instead, he passes easily on to the next matter
of conversation.

Your old acquaintance Londonderry has quietly died at
North Cray! and the virtuous De Witt was torn in pieces
by the populace! What a lucky — the Irishman has been
in his life and end. In him your Irish Franklin *est mort*!

The 'old acquaintance' – the Marquess of Londonderry,
more usually called Lord Castlereagh – was the British Foreign
Minister. If any one man embodied the politics that Shelley

loathed, it was Castlereagh, and each man would have cheerfully welcomed news of the other's death.

It was Castlereagh who forged the military alliances that ended the long Napoleonic Wars and then spent years constructing the subtler machinery of political alliances that would underpin the peace. For the achievement of a peace that lasted, history has praised him. In his lifetime he was widely and warmly loathed. As the man – or, at least, the cat's-paw – who had brought about the abolition of the Irish parliament in which he had once sat, he had been hated for twenty years by all who loved the cause of Ireland's liberty, Shelley not least among them. Castlereagh had committed the deadly constitutional sin of suspending habeas corpus in Ireland. The fact that he had argued at the same time for Catholic emancipation could not redeem him because the king wouldn't have it at any price. Most Irishmen feared and loathed him but, come to that, so did most ordinary Englishmen and they believed the feeling to be mutual. Certainly Castlereagh's zeal in making and enforcing repressive laws let them know that he feared and loathed any proposal that might advance them from political destitution. Shelley's strongest vitriol was reserved for Castlereagh at the time of Peterloo, though what he wrote was not read by Englishmen. Even Hunt was too cautious to print it. Still, by the time of Castlereagh's funeral, it was easy to see and hear that Shelley was only expressing, in better language, the opinions of many. Crowds lined the streets to jeer and cat-call the cortège on its way to the Abbey.

In his letter, Byron seems to be under the impression that Castlereagh had died peacefully at home. He didn't have the facts. Castlereagh, whose mind had collapsed into a black depression, had slit his own throat with a penknife. His death that August must have seemed an auspicious coincidence as the plans to launch the *Liberal* went ahead. For the moment, at least, perhaps feeling himself more, rather than less, under an obligation after Shelley's death, Byron is still on board, and working to enlist Moore.

> Leigh Hunt is sweating articles for his new Journal; and both he and I think it somewhat shabby in *you* not to contribute. Will you become one of the *proper rioters*? 'Do, and we go snacks.' I recommend you to think twice before you respond in the negative.
>
> I have nearly (*quite three*) four new cantos of *Don Juan* ready. I obtained permission from the female Censor Morum of *my* morals to continue it, provided it were immaculate; so I have been as decent as need be. There is a deal of war – a siege, and all that, in the style, graphical and technical, of the shipwreck in Canto Second, which 'took', as they say in the Row.
>
> Yours, etc.
>
> P.S. That — Galignani has about ten lies in one paragraph. It was not a Bible that was found in Shelley's pocket, but John Keats's poems. However, it would not have been strange, for he was a great admirer of Scripture as a composition. *I* did not send my bust to the academy of New York; but I sat for my picture to young West, an American artist, at the request of some members of that Academy to *him* that he would take my portrait, – for the Academy, I believe.

I had, and still have, thoughts of South America, but am fluctuating between it and Greece. I should have gone, long ago, to one of them, but for my liaison with the Countess G[uiccioli]; for love, in these days, is little compatible with glory. *She* would be delighted to go too; but I do not choose to expose her to a long voyage, and a residence in an unsettled country, where I shall probably take a part of some sort.

By the time Byron writes to Mary from Genoa, his meandering journey towards playing that part had begun.

> *Casa Saluzzo, Albaro, Genoa, 6th October, 1822*
>
> . . . I have a particular dislike to anything of Shelley's being within the same walls with Mrs Hunt's children. They are dirtier and more mischievous than Yahoos. What they can't destroy with their filth they will with their fingers. I presume you received ninety and odd crowns from the wreck of the *Don Juan*, and also the price of the boat purchased by Captain R., if not, you will have both. Hunt has these in hand.
>
> With regard to any difficulties about money, I can only repeat that I will be your banker till this state of things is cleared up, and you can see what is to be done; so there is little to hinder you on that score. I was confined for four days to my bed at Lerici. Poor Hunt, with his six little blackguards, are coming slowly up; as usual he turned back once – was there ever such a *kraal* out of the Hottentot country.
>
> N.B.

Shelley's Boat

Byron was laid up at Lerici as a result of exhausting himself trying to outswim Trelawny. He shook of his debility quickly enough but, as much as six months later, he had still not quite shaken off Leigh Hunt and, now, there was no Shelley to temper his exasperation.

To Thomas Moore, Genoa, April 2, 1823

. . . As to Hunt, I prefer *not* having turned him to starve in the streets to any personal honour which might have accrued from some genuine philanthropy. I really act upon principle in this matter, for we have nothing much in common; and I cannot describe to you the despairing sensation of trying to do something for a man who seems incapable or unwilling to do anything further for himself – at least, to the purpose. It is like pulling a man out of a river who directly throws himself in again. For the last three or four years Shelley assisted, and had once actually extricated him. I have since his demise – and even before – done what I could: but it is not in my power to make this permanent . . .

Fifteen

Song to the Men of England

Men of England, wherefore plough
For the lords who lay ye low?
Wherefore weave with toil and care
The rich robes your tyrants wear?

Wherefore feed, and clothe, and save,
From the cradle to the grave,
Those ungrateful drones who would
Drain your sweat – nay, drink your blood?

Wherefore, Bees of England, forge
Many a weapon, chain, and scourge,
That these stingless drones may spoil
The forced produce of your toil?

Have ye leisure, comfort, calm,
Shelter, food, love's gentle balm?
Or what is it ye buy so dear
With your pain and with your fear?

The seed ye sow, another reaps;
The wealth ye find, another keeps;
The robes ye weave, another wears;
The arms ye forge, another bears.

Shelley's Boat

Sow seed, – but let no tyrant reap;
Find wealth, – let no impostor heap;
Weave robes, – let not the idle wear;
Forge arms, – in your defence to bear.

Shrink to your cellars, holes, and cells;
In halls ye deck, another dwells.
Why shake the chains ye wrought? Ye see
The steel ye tempered glance on ye.

With plough and spade, and hoe and loom,
Trace your grave, and build your tomb,
And weave your winding-sheet, till fair
England be your sepulchre.

. . . in youth he had read of 'Illuminati and Eleutherarchs',
and believed that he possessed the power of operating an
immediate change in the minds of men and the state of
society. These wild dreams had faded; sorrow and adversity
had struck home; but he struggled with despondency as he
did with physical pain.

The words come from the notes Mary attached to the poems
of 1817. These days, even among the best-educated, there are
not many who could say with much confidence what an
'eleutherarch' might have been. If you are one of those few,
you will be rewarded with a certain smugness when it comes
up in a crossword, so we can increase the number of smug
crossword-solvers by passing on what the *Shorter Oxford
Dictionary* has to say: 'The chief of an (imaginary) secret
society, "the Eleutheri".' We get a better idea if we go on to:

'Eleutherian: *a. rare*. The title of Zeus as protector of political freedom.'

In suggesting that Shelley had given up the political notions of his youth, Mary is about her work of tidying-up again. He might have outgrown the effervescence of youthful optimism, he might have grown to realise that nobody had the power of operating an immediate change in the minds of men, but he had not abandoned the idea that a poet's job was to change the state of society. His famous definition of poets as 'the unacknowledged legislators of the world' is a simple statement of what he thought his job was. It was to convey an understanding of the deepest, truest laws of human existence and a visionary understanding of what the world and life could be, should it ever be regulated by those laws, rather than laws that amounted to a conspiracy against liberty and a concerted plan to oppress the common man.

There are, strangely enough, many things on which Shelley and Edmund Burke, that great anti-revolutionary, would have agreed. Certainly, Shelley himself might have come up with Burke's declaration that 'bad laws are the worst sort of tyranny'. It was of Burke that Dr Johnson said, 'You could not stand five minutes with that man beneath a shed while it rained but you must be convinced you had been standing with the greatest man you had ever seen,' and, it seems, many people felt much the same on meeting Shelley. That forceful impression of a ceaselessly active mind, the extraordinary fluency of his speech and disconcerting depth and breadth of his knowledge persuaded most who met him that he had some claim to genius.

But there was something simpler that marked him as extraordinary. An assumed public persona was habitual to men and women of rank, just as the wearing of a wig had been, until very lately, the habitual mark of a gentleman. Unlike Byron, who had made an elaborate work of art out of it, Shelley had no assumed persona. He seemed oblivious of how he seemed and oblivious, too, of those distinctions that were thought and taught to be of fundamental importance in a world whose ruling principle was subordination. He was a man who could speak easily and directly, and in the same voice, to any he should chance to meet, irrespective of sex or rank. In face and feature he was so youthful as to be called childlike. His manner, too, was conspicuous for this childlike but not childish quality. It was much of his appeal.

The impression he made on two Scottish ladies, as reported by Trelawny, was not unusual, even if the storyteller has applied his usual wash of colour. They were newly arrived in Pisa, 'fresh from the land of cakes – frank, fair, intelligent and pious'. Trelawny called on them with Shelley in tow but, knowing what pious Scottish ladies had been told to think about the atheistical poet, it was not until later that he told them who his companion had been.

'Shelley! . . . Oh, why did you not name him?'

'Because he thought you would be shocked.'

'Shocked! – Why, I would have knelt to him in penitence for having wronged him in my thoughts. If he is not pure and good then there is not truth and goodness in this world.'

No doubt the sentiment was, indeed, offered by the Scottish ladies, but the opinion Trelawny reports is, emphatically, his own. It provides the light in which Trelawny continually contrasts Shelley with 'cynic Byron', a champion of liberty on the page, a misogynist and a snob in life.

'The truth was,' says Trelawny, 'Shelley loved everything better than himself. Self-preservation is, they say, the first law of nature, with him it was the last; and the only pain he ever gave his friends arose from the utter indifference with which he treated everything concerning himself.'

Even Byron's cynicism was disarmed by Shelley. He wrote to Moore:

> As to poor Shelley, who is another bugbear to you and the world, he is, to my knowledge, the least selfish and the mildest of men – a man who has made more sacrifices of his fortune and feelings for others than any I ever heard of. With his speculative opinions I have nothing in common, nor desire to have.

The 'speculative opinions' in Byron's disclaimer included Shelley's religious or, more to the point, irreligious views but they also included his profoundly radical politics. For all that Byron was ready to rail and jeer at a government made up of men he despised, there is no sign that he believed in the redistribution of wealth on any principle other than personal whim. Liberty for America was one in the eye for his own enemies. Liberty for Greece (or somewhere in South America, say) might be a fine, wild and poetical thing, but liberty for the labouring masses of England or the enslaved and destituted population of Ireland meant political slogging and no romance at all. Worse, it would have cut off most of his income. A cause that threatened his life had attractions. One that might have threatened his privileges had none.

Shelley's Boat

Shelley was different. By the time he died Shelley stood somewhere in the territory between Jeremy Bentham and Karl Marx and, probably, much nearer to the latter. If his own sense of just where in that part of the political spectrum he belonged does not always seem clear, it is worth remembering that the spectrum was a long way from being defined in the way we take for granted today. Shelley died, after all, twenty-six years before Marx published the summary of his socialist ideas as *The Communist Manifesto* and no less than sixty-four years before the appearance of the first English translation of *On Capital*. (And then, only the first volume was to appear. He would have had to live into the twentieth century to see the second and third in English.) Sometimes Shelley seems to be a Benthamite, urging on the benign reconstruction of society through reasonable persuasion and by demonstration of the utility of better ideas. Time and again, though, he finds himself banging his head on the limits of his faith in Benthamite – or Godwinite – gradualism and persuasion. At those times, when the choice lies between pursuing reform by other means or compromising with reaction, he always takes the decisive intellectual step towards revolution. He knows that nothing but insurrection will work.

In 1819, just after Peterloo, Shelley wrote a letter in which he put a question, somewhat disingenuously, to an old friend.

> I wish to ask you if you know of any bookseller who would like to publish a little volume of popular songs wholly political, and destined to awaken and direct the imagination of the reformers. I see you smile – but answer my question.

In a second letter, he wrote:

Shelley's Boat

One thing I want to ask you – do you know any bookseller who would publish for me an octavo volume entitled *A Philosophical View of Reform*? It is boldly, but temperately written, and I think readable. It is intended for a kind of standard book for the philosophical reformers politically considered, like Jeremy Bentham's something, but different and perhaps more systematic. I will send it sheet by sheet. Will you ask and think for me?

Leigh Hunt never replied.

All the same, Shelley wrote a number of the popular songs he spoke of. They include *The Ballad of the Starving Mother* and are written in a language as direct and unvarnished as that title suggests. The educated might have found – might still find – the prosody of these 'popular songs' banal, even risible. Shelley would not have cared. He was writing for the kind of men and women who had their heads broken on St Peter's Field.

Word of 'the massacre' – eleven were killed, many injured – reached Shelley in Livorno on the 5th of September 1819. Apart from those letters to Hunt, his response was *The Mask of Anarchy*, a splendidly savage attack on the administration. By Anarchy, of course, he meant the principles of government that Lords Eldon, Sidmouth and Castlereagh called 'God and King and Law' and that most of us today would call tyranny. Peterloo was the stimulus for a burst of extraordinary incandescence, during which he wrote also his satire on Wordsworth, *Peter Bell The Third*, much of *Prometheus* and what may be the best defence of free speech in the English language, his *Letter on Richard Carlile*. Neither Carlile himself, nor that vindication of him that Shelley was inspired to write, are nearly as well known as they deserve to be. Carlile was, to begin with, a tinsmith by trade. He had none of Leigh Hunt's advantages of education and little of his gift as a writer but he made himself into an even braver and more determined 'bookseller'. All of which meant, alas, that he was in jail when Shelley wrote that fishing letter to Hunt. While he was inside, Carlile's wife – she had lately separated from him but, doughty woman that she was, saw no reason to separate herself from the cause – continued to publish the *Republican* until she, too, was put away. Her sister then took up the work and she, in turn, was put behind bars. The result of this foolish heavy-handedness was that the *Republican*'s circulation grew until it was selling more copies than *The Times*. The government came up with a new tactic. They stuck a tax of fourpence on cheap newspapers and set a minimum price for their sale of sevenpence, an impossibly extravagant amount for a working man in 1819.

Repressive regimes may be able to extinguish the freedom of the press but they can never succeed in silencing the powerful medium of the popular song. Carlile would have found nothing patronising or banal in Shelley's deliberate simplicity. If you are going to get your head broken in the name of Freedom, it's best to have a clear, simple statement of what freedom means, not in some world of hypothesis and abstraction but in the here and now, in words you can still remember after being concussed. Shelley gives it.

> Thou art clothes and fire and food
> For the trampled multitude.

Shelley's Boat

No, in countries that are free
Such starvation cannot be
As in England now we see.

Shelley's curious and high-pitched voice was often remarked on. To hear how good these lyrics really are, sing them in your best Bob Dylan impersonation. Dylan's has certainly been the more audible voice over these past two centuries. Most of these political songs of Shelley's, together with *A Philosophical View of Reform*, found no publisher for nearly two centuries and did not appear in print until 1990.

Sixteen

Shelley's heart resisted the fire. An American doctor of literary interests has suggested that this may indicate a calcifying condition that would explain Shelley's variable health and strange pains. Whatever the reason, the poet's heart endured the flames, recognisably, long after his brains had boiled away. It had been the sound of the mattock striking the skull that had ended the search for his body, and that mattock had knocked in the temples. Those who had the stomach for it, therefore, were able to view the seething in the cauldron of Shelley's skull. This was the sight that put an end to Byron's affectation of insouciance and made him quit the beach for that swim. It is not surprising that after the burning, the party retired to Viareggio and drank heavily. Trelawny attended his furnace to the end without flinching, and seeing the heart still unconsumed, snatched it from the ashes and the glowing iron. It cost him a serious burn. Hunt, pleading his ancient friendship, begged the heart from Trelawny and got it. Mary, who was not there to see the burning, learned of it later and begged the heart from Hunt. It became the subject of an unworthy little tug-of-war. Hunt had it. Hunt, as far as Hunt was concerned, had the better claim to it and he was going to keep it. Mary got the relic in the end but it is hard to think well of Hunt for being so churlish about yielding up his grisly prize.

The heart Trelawny snatched from the furnace – the heart that 'would not take the flames' – was, by his and Mary's and many another account, a great and generous heart with a remarkable capacity for altruism. The Lord Chancellor had taken another view, as we know, classing it a thoroughly wicked heart. After his death, Mary could find nothing blameable in her late espoused saint but she had not been so unequivocal in life.

> My dearest Mary, wherefore hast thou gone,
> And left me in this weary world alone?
> Thy form is here indeed – a lovely one –
> But thou art fled, gone down the dreary road,
> That leads to sorrow's most obscure abode . . .

So he had written to her in 1819 but, in truth, he should have known 'wherefore' she had gone off down that 'dreary road'. She had been sunk in this depression since Clara had died on the terrible journey to Venice the year before. Even if he were beyond the reach of any notion that he might be to blame for what happened – and his so much treasured poet's heart should not have been – that 'wherefore' is astonishing. By it we are to know that the lamentable thing about her sorrow is that he is left 'in this weary world alone'. Some heart. He writes to her again, that same year:

> The world is dreary
> And I am weary
> Of Wandering on without thee, Mary;
> A joy was erewhile
> In thy voice and in thy smile
> And 'tis gone, when I should be gone, too, Mary.

If he has tears, he sheds them for himself. Halfway through

the year in which he wrote those lines, the next blow fell. William died.

Mary did not recover from her depression during all their time in Pisa. Being handed the sheets of another Shelley love-adventure, *Epipsychidion*, to write up the fair copies can hardly have been therapeutic. Then came Casa Magni and, while Mary was living through a nightmare, Shelley's preoccupations were his boat, his friend's wife and his plans for Hunt's periodical. Shelley's altruism, like Godwin's, was political, philosophical, public and – in a way Godwin's could not be – artistic. He was often ready to put money in other people's pockets but the handing out of money is only a relative of altruism and, often enough, it isn't even that. The real thing starts with being ready to put yourself in other people's shoes. That is not where the strength of Shelley's imagination lay. Still, he was not the ruthless exploiter of men's purses that Godwin was and if he was, as Matthew Arnold called him, 'an ineffectual angel', it was mainly because he wasn't all that good at exploiting men. But it seems he could not help being an exploiter of women. They gave him their hearts easily and he abused the gift. It's not much of a defence that he didn't recognise himself as an abuser, or that he had a fine, unworldly sense of what love ought to be. As a defence it amounts to ignorance of himself and ignorance of the real demands love makes. In his poetry, love is always an adventure or a rapture. He had a good go at forcing it to be these things in life as well. He just seems to have had little idea of what was called for when it wasn't these things. Lord Eldon's judgement – that he was a kind of monster – was, in its way, probably nearer the mark than Mary's, but it wasn't his atheism or radicalism that undermined his fitness to be father of his own children. He simply belonged to another species. The species known as Great Artist is, by definition, a kind of monster. It is unlike the rest of us. It is not inevitably bad but it inevitably has its own ideas of what is good. Those ideas are subordinate to its one imperative good, its own art. The necessary intensity of its own self-absorption makes the species only rarely capable of great love. And then it must be after its own fashion and on its own terms. Even through all the monster's selfishness, though, it needs to be loved. And it can be. Who would know that better than the definitive monster-creator, Mary Shelley?

There is at least a glimpse of a Shelley who does know those banal things not proper to genuine monsters, guilt and remorse. There had been times when his conscience called up the shade of Harriet Westbrook. Some burden of calcified guilt on her account lay in that unconsumed heart. It came out to Thomas Love Peacock, a man Shelley trusted enough to be executor of his will, who acted as his literary agent through the years of exile and had been the most necessary of his friends in those damp days back in Marlow.

> I was walking with him in Bisham Wood, and we had been talking in the usual way of our ordinary subjects, when he suddenly fell into a gloomy reverie. I tried to rouse him out of it, and made some remarks which I thought might make him laugh at his own abstraction. Suddenly he said to me, still with the same gloomy expression: 'There is one thing to which I have decidedly made up my mind. I will take a great glass of ale every night.' I said, laughingly,

'A very good resolution, as the result of a melancholy musing.' 'Yes,' he said, 'but you do not know why I take it. I shall do it to deaden my feelings; for I see that those who drink ale have none.' The next day he said to me, 'You must have thought me very unreasonable yesterday evening?' I said, 'I did, certainly.' 'Then,' he said, 'I will tell you what I would not tell anyone else. I was thinking of Harriet.' I told him I had no idea of such a thing; it was so long since he had named her.

The defenders of Shelley's humanity would have pointed out that generous habit of his with money. We may point out that it was money that came to him entirely without labour on his part. He knew perfectly well whose labour put it into his hands. He'd been busy encouraging them to revolt, after all:

> Men of England, wherefore plough
> For the lords who lay ye low?
> Wherefore weave with toil and care
> The rich robes your tyrants wear?
>
> Wherefore feed, and clothe, and save,
> From the cradle to the grave,
> Those ungrateful drones who . . .

And so on.

He lived all his life on the allowance apportioned from the rents that Men of England, busily ploughing, coughed up to the baronet, his father, every quarter-day. He might have denied being an 'ungrateful drone' and in his political philosophy he could justly claim to be the enemy of tyranny but, by his own philosophy, was this money his to give? How justly did he treat the Men of England when he poured away their extorted sweat into the pockets of the money-lenders by way of those post-obit bonds? A pleasure-yacht costing eighty pounds or more surely counted as a rich enough robe according to the principles of his *Philosophical View of Reform*. Wherefore should the Men of England pay for this? Trelawny quotes Mary's remark, 'Many have suggested and advocated far greater innovations in our political and social system than Shelley; but he alone practised those he approved of as just.'

Well, up to a point.

It is not especially blameable that he lived by the standards of his time while thinking ahead of them. Before we accuse him of hypocrisy we might consider our own case. We talk much of freedom in the West, of free markets and free trade and free movement of labour; of freedom of speech and freedom of association. We then clothe ourselves, amuse ourselves and equip our homes with things we can afford in profusion because they are made so cheaply somewhere in the East, by people who don't enjoy these freedoms at all. Western corporations insist on the virtues of 'freeing up the labour market', when what this really means, in many cases, is moving the work to China, where there is nothing remotely like a free market in labour, where workers are, by any reasonable definition, conscripted and where an eighteen-hour day for wages tallied in cents is commonplace. It is not for us to accuse Shelley of hypocrisy, or use the charge to make us comfortable in dismissing his radical indignation. All the same, given that he thought himself a philosopher before he was a poet, we might well think it odd that he did not remark with some embarrassment on the contradiction between his life and his philosophy.

Seventeen

In one pocket a volume of Keats, dead barely a year. In the other, Sophocles, dead two thousand years, whose words Shelley had once quoted to Peacock, while brandishing the little bottle of laudanum that he claimed he was never parted from.

> Man's happiest lot is not to be:
> And when we tread life's thorny steep,
> Most blest are they who earliest free
> Descend to death's eternal sleep.

The ancient poet's thought was alive in his mind when he set himself to write *Adonais*, the elegy for Keats that is also his dialogue with himself concerning – with uncannily prophetic touches – his own death.

> The One remains, the many change and pass;
> Heaven's light forever shines, Earth's shadows fly;
> Life, like a dome of many-coloured glass,
> Stains the white radiance of Eternity,
> Until Death tramples it to fragments. – Die,
> If thou wouldst be with that which thou dost seek!
> Follow where all is fled! – Rome's azure sky,
> Flowers, ruins, statues, music, words are weak
> The glory they transfuse with fitting truth to speak.

Shelley's Boat

Why linger, why turn back, why shrink, my Heart?
Thy hopes are gone before: from all things here
They have departed; thou shouldst now depart!
A light is passed from the revolving year,
And man, and woman; and what still is dear
Attracts to crush, repels to make thee wither.
The soft sky smiles, – the low wind whispers near:
'Tis Adonais calls! Oh, hasten thither,
No more let Life divide what Death can join together.

. . .

The breath whose might I have invoked in song
Descends on me; my spirit's bark is driven
Far from the shore, far from the trembling throng,
Whose sails were never to the tempest given;
The massy earth and sphered skies are riven!
I am borne darkly, fearfully, afar;
Whilst burning through the inmost veil of Heaven,
The soul of Adonais, like a star,
Beacons from the abode where the Eternal are.

Wherever the soul of Adonais could be said to dwell, all that remained of the mortal Keats lay in the Protestant cemetery of the Eternal City. *Roma, Roma, Roma! non e piu com' era prima.* For the Shelleys Rome had become a different place since they had buried William there in that same cemetery. If Shelley had foreseen that he was destined to join his son and his fellow poet there, then the thought had not dismayed him.

The English burying-place [he wrote to Peacock] is a green slope near the walls, under the pyramidal tomb of Cestius, and is, I think, the most beautiful and solemn cemetery I ever beheld. To see the sun shining on its bright grass, fresh, when we first visited it, with the autumnal dews, and hear the whispering of the wind among the leaves of the trees which have overgrown the tomb of Cestius, and the soil which is stirring in the sun-warm earth, and to mark the tombs, mostly of women and young people who were buried there, one might, if one were to die, desire the sleep they seem to sleep. Such is the human mind, and so it peoples with its wishes vacancy and oblivion.

If Shelley had expressed, in that letter to Peacock, a half-formed wish to lie next to William, it had become wholly Mary's wish for the disposal of the ashes. Trelawny attended to this business, too. Delayed in Livorno, he sent the ashes ahead to the British Consul at Rome to await his coming. When he arrived, he found that the Consul had been obliged to complete the funeral and bury the ashes 'with the usual ceremonies' in order 'to quiet the authorities'. Trelawny had no trouble finding the newly turned plot where the Consul had laid the remains to rest and no trouble, either, finding a much better spot altogether. Shelley's remains would lie more fittingly, he saw, in the embrasure formed by two buttresses of the ancient Roman wall that partly enclosed the cemetery. As for the notion of interring the father beside the son, it seems that, although so little time had passed between their deaths, nobody could find the spot where William lay. A few scudi in the palm of the gatekeeper were the only formality observed when it came to digging up Shelley's casket. Trelawny leant his own hand to digging the new grave and masons were soon found to erect a fitting tomb. The niche, Trelawny mentions, 'suited my taste' and, oddly enough, it was big enough to hold not one but two tombs. 'The other tomb was built merely to fill up the recess,' Trelawny says. 'I planted eight seedling cypresses. When I last saw them in 1844, the seven which remained were about thirty-five feet in height. I added flowers as well. The ground I had purchased, I enclosed, and so ended my task.'

The second tomb was not built just to fill up the space at all. Trelawny, being Trelawny, palms off this transparent fib without a blush. It was, of course, for himself. He was the one who was to lie next to Shelley for eternity, though he did later mention to Mary that he thought there was some adjacent space available should she want a plot for herself. Sixty years were to pass, all but, before the time came when, according to his instructions, Trelawny's body was shipped to Gotha, there to be cremated, and his ashes taken on to Rome. There they were laid in that neighbour tomb to Shelley's in the shade of the seven cypresses. A beautiful plan, beautifully fulfilled. Not that it matters, but just a little murmur of a question comes to mind. Was William's grave really impossible to find? Had that palm-crossed custodian really, as one might say, completely lost the plot? Or did his gnarled old finger point out some inconvenient yard-and-a-half in a crowded corner without, well, room for a decent tomb or two and the odd Cornishman here or there?

Eighteen

'Lord Byron ist nur grosse wann er dichtet. Als bald er reflektiert, er ist ein kind.' Lord Byron is only great as far as poetry is concerned. As soon as he starts thinking, he is a but a child. That was Goethe's opinion. It was also, more or less, Trelawny's, to which he adds that anything of Byron's that seems like a strenuous thought is more than likely due to the influence, instruction or conversation of Shelley. Whatever the truth of that, it is true that Shelley's opinion was not all that far from Goethe's. He admired Byron's soaring talent but only wished his aim were as lofty. He wished, for instance, that the bestseller Byron were less attentive to the public taste and what would 'take'. 'Write nothing but what your conviction of its truth inspires you to write,' Shelley told Byron. 'Time will reverse the judgement of the vulgar. Contemporary criticism only represents the amount of ignorance genius has to contend with.'

A resurrected Shelley, then, might feel vindicated to find that he has readers in the twenty-first century, after all, and many, many more of them than he ever had in life. He might, on the other hand, be a little dismayed to find that 'eleutherarchy' is not much discussed. He would be even more dismayed and certainly puzzled to learn that, after a century and a quarter of free, universal and compulsory education, few people read poetry and almost nobody ever reads a poem longer than a page. It is something of a mystery. If you are reading this at all, then you are probably more than usually interested in literature. Yet if everybody in your acquaintance who has read the whole of *Prometheus Unbound* and *The Revolt of Islam* were to send you a pound, you would be lucky to raise the price of a sandwich and a cup of coffee. If you're confident you would also be able to leave a tip, you have unusual friends. If you think you'd have enough for a dinner, you live in a literary stratosphere. Yet, for Shelley and for those who believed in him, his great work lay in those very poems that the general reader now finds far too long to be digestible. It is in these more strenuous works that the 'unacknowledged' legislation of the poet is to be found. The fact that *Ozymandias* is in every anthology and is among the most quoted lines of verse in the English language would not console Shelley much for the fact that nobody reads *Prometheus Unbound* or that many, perhaps most, of those who can quote a line or so from the 'Ode to the West Wind' ('If Winter comes, can Spring be far behind?') think the Ode is about the west wind rather than liberty.

If Shelley had lived in our world, where the monuments of Rameses are pictured on a million postcards, he might well have scribbled 'Ozymandias' on the back of one, posted the thing and forgotten about it. (Though Mary would have made a copy.) He would certainly have recognised that the poem's central thought, however well expressed, is a commonplace. Such verses were, for him, hardly more than a compulsive poet's form of notes and messages and exclamations. They were expressions of his momentary feelings, responses, needs and pains. They show us his heart. They are not where he would send us to look for his mind. That we leave *Queen Mab* to moulder but will not let such trifles as his poems to Jane Williams die would astonish him. It would astonish, too, the Chartists or the followers of the proto-socialist Robert Owen, who quoted it as others might quote the Bible.

It is hard to argue with the 'ineffectual angel' judgement but, then, since Shelley died, no poet has arisen with anything comparable to his ambitions, effectual or not. Browning and Tennyson, over much longer lives, were as productive but do not compare in moral or political passion. Tennyson – it was his own verdict on himself – simply had nothing much to say, only a wonderful faculty for saying it. He flattered the world he lived in so well that it made a lord of him. If Browning had greater ambitions than Tennyson, despite his besetting sin of flippancy, they were private rather than public in nature. He did much to set poetry on the course that, for the most part, it has been on ever since, towards becoming the local journalism of the poet's soul and surrounding district, too often a rather small beat. That shift has gone hand in hand with the long decline in the public importance of poetry since the wreck of *Ariel*. There are many reasons for that decline and, as is the way with history, reasons that beget reasons, but one of them may be that when the little boat went down it took with it the last poet who truly, madly, deeply believed that poetry was important enough to change the world.

Nineteen

The lovely, if unloved, *Bolivar* went to Lord Blessington for four hundred guineas. When all the bills were in, it was less than half of what she had cost, so Blessington should have been well content with his bargain. He did not get, and perhaps did not want, the chairs with Byron's crest on them. Byron kept those. He kept the two brass cannon as well. They went into the armoury that was then shipped aboard the altogether less rakish but more capacious brig he had hired for his expedition to join the War of Greek Independence. When Trelawny, who chose to throw his lot in with the venture, clapped eyes on *Hercules*, he was not impressed, not even when Byron explained that he had been able to get her on very easy terms. A poor bargain at any price, was Trelawny's opinion. She was an old tub, 'collier-built', ill-prepared and a poor sailor. She was all that was to be had in Genoa, said Byron. 'Leghorn is the place for shipping,' said Trelawny.

'Why, then did you not come here sooner? I had no one to help me.'

'You had Captain Roberts, the very man for the occasion. We might as well have built a raft . . . '

Trelawny was being disingenuous. He well knew that Roberts had offered his advice and Byron had not taken it. He knew, too, that Captain Roberts, by this time, was fed up to the back teeth with Byron and wanted no more to do with him. Among the last straws had been a peevish correspondence from Byron about small items in the *Bolivar* accounts. The particular item he wanted Roberts to account for, or to show the money for, was a quantity of iron ballast that seems to have been surplus to requirements. The wildly extravagant are often niggardly over trifles and few men showed it as exasperatingly as Byron. Still, had Edward Williams, the sailor, been as nit-pickingly observant in accounting for every last lump of iron ballast as was Byron, the landlubber, he might not have shrugged off a three-inch shift in his waterline as a matter of evaporation.

The noble ideal of Hellenic freedom may or may not have been uppermost in Byron's mind as he planned what was to be his own fatal voyage. (' . . . I had, and still have, thoughts of South America, but am fluctuating between it and Greece . . . ') It was far from being the first or only motive driving the misalliance of Greek warlords, bandits, tricksters and politicians into whose pockets he was about to pour his fortune. Byron was not wholly deluded about all this, even before he embarked on the chaotic enterprise, but what other thing was there for him to do than join their chaotic, but just possibly glorious, enterprise?

Trelawny believed that Byron had never really stopped being that now old-fashioned thing, a Regency buck. He had been – and still is – parcelled up with the radical poets of his age, the 'Romantics', but in truth, even as a poet, he did not belong with his contemporaries. He remained rooted in the age that had gone before, with Swift and Pope long dead. Now even the poets younger than he were dead. At thirty-six, not altogether suddenly, he felt old and tired and remaindered. Heading in the direction of the Greek war was not the same as choosing death but it did offer the chance, at least, of meeting his end, like Shelley, in a halfway decent metaphor. Whether it was wise, with this in mind, to have a helmet fashioned for himself in a fanciful burlesque of the ancient style is debatable. It invites and gets the kind of mockery that you don't want in a terminal metaphor. Still, had he been acclaimed King of the Greeks – and the notion was mentioned – it would have found a place in the regalia. So, a few days after selling *Bolivar* and quizzing Roberts about the unaccounted-for ballast, and with the helmet safely stowed, Byron weighed anchor in Genoa. The fat little brig *Hercules*, that sailed even more lamely than he walked, began her long wallow towards the Ionian and an appointment at Missolonghi. It was an appointment with fever, diarrhoea, the bleeding habits of bad doctors and death, on a fly-blown mudflat on the edge of a swamp. The ridiculous helmet stayed in its box. There would be no limelight.

As for *Ariel*, after salvaging her, Roberts repaired the damage. Wisely, he gave her a deck and probably a little more ballast. I have found no record of what he did to the sail plan, but his was bound to be more conservative than Williams's exciting spread of sail. There, after all, lay the heart of all the doubts he'd expressed from the beginning. Still, she was wrecked again.

'Roberts possessed himself of her, and decked her,' wrote Mary, editing the first collected edition of Shelley's poems in 1839, 'but she proved not seaworthy, and her shattered planks now lie rotting on the shore of one of the Ionian islands, on which she was wrecked.'

She had gone down with the poet who had called her

Shelley's Boat

Ariel. Then, it seems, she had been resurrected and, some-how or other, followed the poet who had called her *Don Juan*, only to mimic his fate by dying, once and for all, on some unimportant interruption of the Ionian coast. Extraordinary that it should have been the 'Ionian islands'. You might almost think Mary invented or adjusted that detail. Though she draws no attention to it, she cannot have been blind or deaf to a certain poetry in this last image of *Ariel.* For, if she met her end in the Ionian, then *Ariel*'s final voyage turns into the little ghost-ship's fulfilment of the vision in *Epipsychidion*:

> Emily,
> A ship is floating in the harbour now,
> A wind is hovering o'er the mountain's brow;
> There is a path on the sea's azure floor,
> No keel has ever plough'd that path before;
> The halcyons brood around the foamless isles;
> The treacherous Ocean has forsworn its wiles;
> The merry mariners are bold and free:
> Say, my heart's sister, wilt thou sail with me?
> Our bark is as an albatross, whose nest
> Is a far Eden of the purple East;
> And we between her wings will sit, while Night,
> And Day, and Storm, and Calm, pursue their flight,
> Our ministers, along the boundless Sea,
> Treading each other's heels, unheededly.
> It is an isle under Ionian skies,
> Beautiful as a wreck of Paradise,
> And, for the harbours are not safe and good,

Shelley's Boat

This land would have remain'd a solitude
But for some pastoral people native there,
Who from the Elysian, clear, and golden air
Draw the last spirit of the age of gold,
Simple and spirited; innocent and bold.
The blue Aegean girds this chosen home,
With ever-changing sound and light and foam,
Kissing the sifted sands, and caverns hoar;
And all the winds wandering along the shore
Undulate with the undulating tide:
There are thick woods where sylvan forms abide;
And many a fountain, rivulet, and pond,
As clear as elemental diamond,
Or serene morning air; and far beyond,
The mossy tracks made by the goats and deer
(Which the rough shepherd treads but once a year)
Pierce into glades, caverns and bowers, and halls
Built round with ivy, which the waterfalls
Illumining, with sound that never fails
Accompany the noonday nightingales;
And all the place is peopled with sweet airs;
The light clear element which the isle wears
Is heavy with the scent of lemon-flowers,
Which floats like mist laden with unseen showers,
And falls upon the eyelids like faint sleep;
And from the moss violets and jonquils peep
And dart their arrowy odour through the brain
Till you might faint with that delicious pain.
And every motion, odour, beam and tone,
With that deep music is in unison:

Shelley's Boat

Which is a soul within the soul – they seem
Like echoes of an antenatal dream.
It is an isle 'twixt Heaven, Air, Earth and Sea,
Cradled and hung in clear tranquillity;
Bright as that wandering Eden Lucifer,
Wash'd by the soft blue Oceans of young air.
It is a favour'd place. Famine or Blight,
Pestilence, War and Earthquake, never light
Upon its mountain-peaks; blind vultures, they
Sail onward far upon their fatal way:
The wingèd storms, chanting their thunder-psalm
To other lands, leave azure chasms of calm
Over this isle, or weep themselves in dew,
From which its fields and woods ever renew
Their green and golden immortality.

```
┌─────────────────────────────────────┐
│ ┌─────────────────────────────────┐ │
│ │                                 │ │
│ │     PERCY BYSSHE SHELLEY        │ │
│ │                                 │ │
│ │        COR CORDIUM             │ │
│ │                                 │ │
│ │    NATUS IV AUG MDCCXCII       │ │
│ │                                 │ │
│ │   OBIIT VIII JUL MDCCCXXII     │ │
│ │                                 │ │
│ │   Nothing of him that doth fade │ │
│ │   But doth suffer a sea-change  │ │
│ │   Into something rich and strange. │
│ │                                 │ │
│ └─────────────────────────────────┘ │
└─────────────────────────────────────┘
```

Inscription on Shelley's gravestone in the Protestant Cemetery in Rome. The Latin COR CORDIUM translates as HEART OF HEARTS. The verse comes from the song sung by Ariel in *The Tempest* (Act 1, Scene 2).